T0158305

CHEMICAL KHICHDI

Aparna Piramal Raje is a writer, columnist, public speaker, educator and adviser who likes to connect the dots and explore the intersections between diverse disciplines. Leadership, business, design, workplaces, education and mental health are her overlapping areas of interest. She attributes her interest in multidisciplinary thinking to her time as a student at the University of Oxford and Harvard Business School.

Her column 'Head Office', in *Mint*, looks at leadership through the blended lens of workspace design and management workstyles. The column led to her first book, *Working Out of the Box*. She has also examined the confluence of the many forces that shape our cities, for newspapers such as the UK's *Financial Times Weekend*.

A visiting faculty member at the Anant National University in Ahmedabad, she teaches a module called 'Netflix and the Art of Design Writing' and serves on the university's board of studies. Aparna enjoys speaking on design, leadership and business in various forums, including industry associations, companies and business schools. Coming from a family of Lego enthusiasts, she is a trained Lego Serious Play facilitator.

She is an adviser to Wonder Girls, a learning platform for adolescent girls, and Talk to Me, a mental health NGO. With the publication of *Chemical Khichdi*, Aparna seeks to leverage her lived experience to contribute to India's mental health landscape. She invites you to visit her website, www.aparnapiramalraje.com, and connect with her on social media.

ALSO BY THE SAME AUTHOR

Working Out of the Box

Business Mantras (co-authored with Gita Piramal,
Radhika Piramal and Mukesh Beriwala)

ADVANCE PRAISE FOR THE BOOK

'Brain-related mental health issues affect the large majority of families. Unfortunately, many of these conditions remain misunderstood and are painfully debilitating and life-altering. While these conditions aren't new, they remain underfunded from a research perspective and yet are more treatable with advances in science and therapies. This personalized experience reveals how mental health conditions affect us as individuals, caregivers, allies or colleagues and explains why we should pay more attention to these challenges as a society. This is an especially valuable read for our post-pandemic, new-normal world'—**Richard A. Friedman, chairman, asset management division, Goldman, Sachs & Co, co-chairman, The Mount Sinai Health System, and founder, Friedman Brain Institute, The Mount Sinai Health System, New York**

'Mental health has often been looked at through the lens of individuals and families. In this poignant memoir, Aparna rightly draws attention to workplace mental health, alongside the role of doctors, family and other allies. I believe there are profound societal, human and economic benefits of taking workplace mental health seriously. A most valuable read for anyone leading an organization today, even if they are new to mental health concerns'—**Punit Renjen, global CEO, Deloitte**

'*Chemical Khichdi* is an inspiring story of vulnerability and resilience, whether or not one has a mental health condition. It offers valuable lessons in different aspects of one's personal and professional life. I found the reference to mental health in the workplace particularly compelling, as that is a very significant, and often overlooked, aspect of our mental health and well-being. A useful and timely read'
—**N. Chandrasekaran, chairman, Tata Sons**

'I applaud Aparna's strength and resilience to want to fight her illness and lead a productive life. Having been in this field for some time, I know the daily struggles and the fortitude one needs to face and fight mental health conditions. She is a true warrior and a hero! A powerful and authentic account of lived experience with a mental health condition, I am sure *Chemical Khichdi* will spread much-needed awareness and help many others facing similar challenges'—**Neerja Birla, founder and chairperson, Aditya Birla Education Trust**

'"Courage" comes from the Latin word "cor", meaning "heart". Aparna has shared her story with great heart and openness, and this is a must-read for individuals and families who have dealt with mental health issues. Having had depression (and solved through talk therapy) in my twenties, I found Aparna's book to have a very practical and strong toolkit on what you can do to get and stay healthy. Thank you, Aparna, for your infinite courage and for writing this wonderful book'—**Nisaba Godrej, executive chairperson, Godrej Consumer Products Ltd**

'It takes enormous courage to write about one's own mental health problems and it takes enormous storytelling skills to do it well. Aparna Piramal Raje has shown both of these in her book, *Chemical Khichdi*. A very interesting and informative book—a must-read for all who value mental health'—**Shekhar Saxena, Professor of the Practice of Global Mental Health, Harvard T.H. Chan School of Public Health, Harvard University**

'Aparna gives a poignant and very real account of her bipolar journey thus far and she thoughtfully shares insights on her progression to approaching her mental health from a holistic perspective that truly allows her to thrive. She goes beyond the work of destigmatization through the way she treats herself with grace and non-judgement in these pages, modelling this for those with bipolar and their loved ones. She shares pearls of life wisdom that will surely resonate with all'—**Kristin S. Raj, MD, clinical assistant professor, co-section chief, Mood Disorders, and chief, Bipolar Clinic, Department of Psychiatry and Behavioral Sciences, Stanford University School of Medicine**

For
Vitamin Rads
Amartya & Agastya
And the sibling bond
With love, hugs and gratitude

Foreword

A t first glance, Aparna's life looks ideal. Raised in Mumbai and London, she studied at Oxford University and Harvard Business School. A popular columnist with the *Mint*, a leading business daily in India, she has previously contributed to the UK's *Financial Times Weekend*, and is a published author, with growing interests in education and philanthropy. A former chief executive of a leading furniture business and from a well-known Indian business family, she is married with two children.

Only close friends and family members know that she has struggled with a serious mental illness for over twenty years—bipolar disorder. I have known Aparna and her family for several decades. I have seen her grow and mature, from an energetic teenager to a curious young adult and now a multitasking mother. I have witnessed her bipolarity, her oscillations and mood swings, and observed how she, with the support of her family, has learnt to live with a sometimes-volatile mind, one that can have too much of a life of its own. *Chemical Khichdi* compiles stories and insights from her personal lived experience in an honest and authentic way.

Aparna has shared her illness, her vulnerabilities and her steps to recovery without holding back. I salute her courage and her resolve to help others.

There has never been a better time to share this story. Mental health concerns are a global pandemic. These once-invisible challenges are becoming ever more visible today. Individual stories might vary, from elite athletes who take time off from competing to take care of their mental health, to recurring tragedies of young people who die by suicide or the everyday stresses and anxieties at home and in the workplace because of Covid-19. Whatever the circumstances, the message is the same: mental health affects our well-being as much as physical health.

The statistics on mental health are overwhelming and can seem bleak. 'Two of the most common mental health conditions, depression and anxiety, cost the global economy US$ 1 trillion each year,' says the World Health Organization (WHO).[1] Approximately one billion people globally experienced a mental or a substance use disorder in 2017, estimates *Our World In Data*, an online scientific publication.[2] And 'more than 8 in 10 people with mental health problems in low-income countries receive no help,' says the World Economic Forum.[3] These challenges have a universal footprint, with a devastating multiplier impact, affecting individuals, families, companies, economies and nations.

Yet *Chemical Khichdi* is a story of hope.

Its 'seven therapies to promote mental health and well-being' present a pathway for everyone—individuals, family members, friends, colleagues and well-wishers—to cope, survive and heal. To nourish ourselves and our loved ones in a holistic and nurturing way. This book is as much for caregivers as it is for those dealing with a mental health condition themselves. After all, each one of us knows someone, in our respective inner circles, who is battling a mental health condition of some sort.

At a time when mental health matters so much, but remains so misunderstood, Aparna's story reinforces that you can live with a vulnerability without becoming its victim. That you can live your life on your terms, even if you've been dealt a tough hand. And indeed, that our deepest vulnerabilities can be transformed into our biggest strengths, prompting us to re-examine our most fundamental notions of success and happiness. It is a message that needs to be shared as widely and as visibly as possible.

Anand Mahindra,
Non-Executive Chairperson,
Mahindra Group

Introduction

I have lived with bipolarity—classified as a serious mental illness—for over two decades. I believe that you can have a mental health condition and raise a family, be in stable, loving and supportive relationships with close family and friends, study at leading educational institutions, turn around a company, write a book and a popular column, teach students, give a little back to society, travel around the world, fail at learning the piano and fall off a horse and get back on it again . . .

In other words, you can be happy, successful and bipolar, whatever your dreams. That's the message of this book. It aspires to be hopeful and helpful. This is why I reveal my vulnerability in all its misshapen glory. There are about half a dozen very good reasons not to do so. Radical transparency, such as this, is not an easy decision. But I hope it helps change the perception of bipolarity and mental health conditions in general.

Whilst I have occasionally been incapacitated by my condition, most of the time I am 'normal'. Who really knows what normal is? But for me, it means that I am on top of my thoughts, more or less, and not the other way around. 'Therapies' enable me to keep myself together. Not fancy New Age therapies, but therapies drawn from real life, from real people. These certainly include conventional medical therapies—psychotherapy and drug therapy—but go beyond them.

My definition of therapies seeks to be holistic and includes medical therapy, love therapy, the therapy of empathy, self-therapy, work therapy, spiritual therapy and lifestyle therapy. Individually, each of them forms a chapter and collectively they form my protective scaffolding. These therapies have helped me lessen the highs and the lows, and maintain and prolong periods of equilibrium. These therapies are not cures; I live with the knowledge that I can veer into mania or depression any time, but they are important daily therapeutic practices.

The book is in three parts. The first section is a memoir, chronicling my story over the last twenty years. The second section consists of the seven therapies—my mental health 'hacks'—and leans towards self-help. And the final and concluding section looks to the future, with reflections on mental health and on new therapies. Both sections one and two contain many interviews with those in my ecosystem, as well as those outside my orbit.

I would like to take this opportunity to elaborate a bit more on the seven therapies, which are not exhaustive. After many years of struggling with frequent manic episodes, I experienced a few years of 'planetary alignment', when these therapies seemed to coalesce, when the stabilizing factors in my life seemed to unite. Yet it is by no means necessary that you need all seven therapies to cope and heal. They simply represent a template of options that can be personalized, depending on one's preferences. For me, medical therapies, love therapy and lifestyle therapy represent a troika that is quite essential for anyone with any mental health condition. Other chapters—allies and the therapy of empathy, work therapy, spiritual therapy and self-therapy—might be more or less relevant, depending on one's personal inclinations.

The chapters also symbolize parallel journeys, not a sequential path to recovery. Each chapter is a self-contained story in itself.

Therapies need therapists and I am blessed with many individuals who have responded when I have reached out to them. From medical practitioners to family members, friends, mentors, work colleagues, fellow readers and writers, spiritual teachers, allies and more, I have tried to include as many voices as I could in this book. Mental health is, after all, a team sport. These interviews hold a mirror to my progress and evolution, provide real-time insights into how best to manage a mental health condition and capture the valuable role of many assorted stakeholders.

Readers will notice that there are also several references to external individuals, start-ups and non-profits in the mental health space. This is my attempt to provide additional resources to the reader and should not be interpreted as an endorsement of any one organization over another. By blending memoir, self-help and reportage, I hope to make this book as helpful as possible to readers.

A quick word on nomenclature—I have referred to individuals in this book as I do so in regular conversation and communication. For example, friends are referred to by their first names, work colleagues by their full names and family elders with their respective 'titles'. In cases where two individuals share the same name, I have included surnames to avoid confusion. No names have been changed, except in a couple of instances.

A note also on terminology: there is a debate about whether one should say 'I am bipolar' or 'I have bipolar'—the latter, to my mind, seems grammatically incorrect. I prefer saying 'I am bipolar' or 'I live with bipolarity', and that I have a mental health condition, rather than a disorder, which, to me, suggests a malfunction of some sort.

Finally, I would like to discuss three important and interrelated aspects of my mental health existence: privilege, stigma and the impact of the pandemic.

I would like to admit upfront that financial issues have not been a challenge for me or my family. As an affluent business family, we have had access to the best medical resources. My mood swings have not been triggered by monetary concerns either—one of the biggest and most universal causes of stress. But, as I describe in some detail, it took me years to get treatment and a few more years to stabilize. Awareness of mental illness is very different now than it was twenty years ago, yet it is nascent and insufficient. My experiences have led me to realize that mental health and illness are fundamental elements of the human condition, cutting across society. Whatever the triggers and the drivers, it is essential to withhold judgement.

The therapies in this book are within reach of individuals and families of varying backgrounds. A list of resources, described in the chapters themselves, as well as at the end of the book, has also been included in order to make mental health services more accessible to readers.

Privilege helps to insulate against stigma, in my experience. No one in my immediate circle has ever made me feel even the slightest bit ashamed of my condition. Whilst there might have been some initial hesitancy about my writing this book, my friends, family and co-workers have been extremely supportive. This is also a luxury that not everyone enjoys. I hope this book makes it easier for those with a mental health condition to be better understood by their loved ones, by enabling loved ones to understand how they might help.

The pandemic has brought mental health to the forefront. Some call it 'the shadow pandemic'. Personally, I found that the first lockdown in 2020 elevated my productivity. Even as I watched the heartbreaking migrant and livelihood crisis, I found the time, space and discipline to work on this manuscript. But the second wave was different. Hearing relentless first-hand stories of personal losses, I felt suffocated, claustrophobic and depressed for several weeks, and my progress was slower.

All of us know those who struggle to cope with Covid-19. The statistics support our empirical findings. Nearly six out of ten therapists who took an online survey said that individuals who had previously recovered or were making a recovery have now relapsed, according to 'COVID-19 Blues: Suicidal Thoughts On The Rise In Youth, Say Therapists', an article on the mental health impact of the pandemic.[1] A similar percentage of therapists said, in the same article,[2] that the number of people they're seeing, who have never sought therapy before, has risen since the outbreak of the pandemic. And 'over 70% of the therapists who participated in the study reported an increase in the number of people who expressed a death wish or suicidal ideation, after the outbreak of COVID-19', says an article about the same study in The Wire, citing anxiety, job loss or fear of job loss, stress, isolation/loneliness and financial insecurity as the most common problems.[3]

Even more reason to focus on mental health.

These seven therapies help me remain stable and recover when I am unwell. They represent years of inner work. I hope they resonate with anyone struggling with mental health challenges and their loved ones. Realistically, that is all of us.

Thank you for taking the time to be part of my journey. I wish you all the best on yours.

Prologue

January 2013, Munger, Bihar

It is about 7 degrees in the coldest month of the year, but my bare toes do not seem to notice it. Nor do I. Why would I care about external details like the weather when my mind is entirely consumed by itself? This is my seventh day at the Bihar School of Yoga ashram in Munger and there is a chaotic symphony of soundtracks in my head.

I arrived at the ashram a week earlier in a volatile state. Triumphant—because the *Mint* newspaper had published my first front-page story, a piece on how a new urban planning initiative in Delhi could lead to better safety for women. Stressed—about whether I could pull off an upcoming urbanization series, which I had worked on for three months, one of the longest by a single byline. Excited—at the thought of staying in an ashram for the first time, exploring an Indian state that often made the headlines for the wrong reasons. Troubled—because of the Nirbhaya gang rape that had occurred a few weeks ago and was still keeping me up at night. Angry—because of the pathetic Delhi state government response to the incident. And more than a little paranoid and fearful—for my safety in a remote part of India.

By day seven, this volatility, combined with lack of sleep, is close to the bipolar equivalent of spontaneous combustion, i.e., mania tinged with psychosis.

At night, I am traumatized by nightmares of the Nirbhaya gang rape, especially the brutalities of the metal rod being inserted into the young woman's body. But now, it is more than just horrific imagery. I am awake, not dreaming. I actually feel like her soul has pierced my consciousness and is making me relive her ordeal whilst I lie on my wooden cot. I feel blood gushing between my legs, the attacks on my body. All I can do to fight the nightmare is chant 'Sitaram' over and over again, until dawn, clinging to the words like a lifeline. This hallucination leads to another delusion—I imagine that a friend has been similarly sexually assaulted and abandoned by a group of men in the past. Unlike 'regular' nightmares that dissolve at daybreak, these delusions haunt me every night and bleed into the day, leaving me distressed and often tearful.

So it is with great relief and enthusiasm that I wake up before dawn and explore the ashram. The white, low-rise buildings are surrounded by large grounds, including grassy lawns for relaxing and open-air gathering sites for prayer and satsanghs. I creep into places I am not meant to, such as a large gathering of foreign devotees, all wearing maroon robes and chanting in Sanskrit, with the morning mist rising. It is a Bernardo Bertolucci film—what better place could there be? I continue to break rules during the day—attempting to go for yoga classes that I hadn't registered for because I couldn't organize myself, unable to complete the mandatory karma yoga assignments, generally making a nuisance of myself.

On one occasion though, I try to contribute to the ashram's upkeep by straightening into neat rows all the slippers and sandals at the entry of the dining hall. When a monk asks me if anyone had requested me to tidy the pile, I mumble something about 'the mess was disturbing the ashram's aesthetic', which was simple but ordered and vibrant, with rows of orange and yellow flowers at regular intervals. I then proceed to challenge some onlookers to do a surya namaskar or two. Just some of the many whims I find myself acting on.

And I dance like never before—at the evening kirtans, freely, spontaneously and mostly, I am told by some members of the audience, quite gracefully, as I search for harmony and beauty to distract myself from my disfigured delusions.

My roommates—one of whom is a friend from Mumbai, Bhairavi, and the other, her friend, whom I had met for the first time on the trip—are flummoxed, because I am quite literally on my own trip. There are so many other people to make friends with and I cannot stop talking to anyone who will listen. I have lunch regularly with a trio of local young men, as we sit cross-legged and eat the wholesome ashram fare, served to us from large steel vats. I take refuge in a couple of maternal-looking women, sharing my fears and nightmares and exchange phone numbers with a lonely old man (He even calls me a few weeks later to make sure that I am feeling better). All of them are subjected to my verbal volley in some shape or form.

Bhairavi was shocked at my behaviour, she tells me much later. 'It was just like a champagne bottle which had gone pop and it was flying out. And the energy was all over. You weren't harnessing it, that was the only thing. But I wish that it had been harnessed because then you may have literally flown, it was so good. I have always seen you as somebody very shy, very gentle and very quiet. For me to see you dancing and chanting is when I realized that there is something that needs to be sorted here. You were in a zone. When you were not part of anything, you were on the phone, constantly. But you couldn't focus, that was the whole irony. The energy was insane. But you were not able to focus.'

Mania makes me lose sight of the mundane. I lose track of which sets of clothes I've worn and which I haven't, grabbing what is closest to my hand every morning. I can't recall bathing much. Directions are impossible. Three days into our trip, I cannot find my way back from the dining room or from the open-air satsangh area to the housing block, even though they are just a few minutes' walk from each other. Bhairavi has to almost grab me by the collar and explain the layout to me and yet I am disoriented.

And although I do not mention it to anyone at the time, by the end of the week, I have voices in my head, imaginary conversations with my friends and mentors that I keep up as a background soundtrack to try and steady a restless mind, one that is darting in all directions. For me, mania is distinguished by a single feature: a background commentary, a parallel line of thinking and feeling that overshadows a normal line of reasoning. When I am not Nirbhaya getting raped, I am an avatar of curious little Krishna exploring the ashram by day or a warrior taking on the world. I am special. I certainly am not Aparna. And I need to communicate that to my mentors, through a telepathic conversation with them.

Towards the end of the programme, I experience a magical moment as I explore the library with stealth and silence, knowing I am not meant to go there. Suddenly, I feel the urge to lie on the ground and I find a spot. I do a series of spontaneous, fluid asanas, moving my limbs as if I'm communing with the universe itself, my body no longer following my command but that of a higher order. This incredible feeling seems to last a good ten minutes or so and ends on its own, leaving me feeling revitalized.

It is one of the most traumatic times of my life, full of paranoia and suspicion. But it is also one of the most exhilarating weeks of my life, full of joy, energy and devotion.

I feel alive like never before, but everyone can see that something is wrong. My bizarre behaviour is only too apparent to the monks and nuns who are observing me. My friends and I have, after all, come to the ashram to strengthen our spiritual practice and cleanse ourselves of toxins, but I seem to be taking them head-on. As the programme is short, our return flights are not easy to change. We are travelling as a trio and it makes sense to stay on until the end.

The week of civil war, with nightmares at night, and fantasy, song and music in the day, ends. We are ready to go back home and just about leave the village near the ashram when we have an accident with a motorcyclist. Angry villagers throw stones and bricks at our vehicle, shattering our windscreen and windows. There we are, three women with limited mobile battery life, with a young driver, in rural Bihar, as the sun is beginning to set.

After driving on the highway for some time, we stop at the nearest village. Distraught, I walk up to a group of women and burst into tears, telling them about the accident. Initially suspicious of who we are, they eventually find a white plastic chair and sit me down in front of a simple one-room home with fields behind it. My friends and the driver are pursuing the sensible path of finding another vehicle that could take us back to the ashram. As for me, in my frenzied state, I am busy making friends with the local children, showing them pictures of my family in Mumbai on my camera, fully prepared to spend the night on my own in a stranger's home in an unknown village. A middle-aged man with a reassuring appearance from the community comes up to me and tries to calm me down, saying, 'I was in the police, don't worry,' as they start making up a bed for me on the porch of the home. You see, I didn't trust our driver after the accident. And it is obvious it is too late to go to Patna.

Bhairavi is fearful for my safety and calls my husband Amit as I insist on staying in the village. Yet common sense eventually prevails. I go back to the ashram with my friends. They leave the next day for Patna, but I am still suspicious of any unknown drivers.

Finally, Amit comes to get me. Direct flights to Patna are cancelled because of the fog and cold weather, so he flies to Kolkata from Mumbai. The overnight Duronto Express from Kolkata to Patna is his only option. With a newspaper to lie down on, he puts his shoes under his head, covers himself with a blanket and sleeps in a third-class, non-reservation compartment, with the winter wind hugging him closely for the next eight hours.

Arup Mukherjee and Punit Kumar, two members of the Patna branch of our family business, VIP luggage, escort me from Munger to Patna, where I meet Amit in a hotel. My hair is a mess, I am unwashed and on a high, with infinite reserves of energy, insisting to him that 'my chakras have opened'. Amit and I take a train to Kolkata and fly back to Mumbai, one of his most difficult trips as he tries to contain my energy in a sealed compartment.

This is not the first time that a family member has had to come to my rescue. But Patna is a milestone. That's when we realize as a family—this needs immediate medical attention.

● ● ●

Part I: The Condition

In the past I've been willing to attribute the timing of these episodes to specific events, but now I feel I need to confront the reality that this is a 'condition' or a 'tendency' I'm going to have to navigate for the rest of my life. Whose approval am I seeking? What recognition do I crave? How important is professional achievement for personal happiness? And what is the narrative of my life that I'm comfortable with?

June 2012
(extract from journal)

1

Un-Diagnosis
(2000–2012)

I was born in Mumbai on 5 February 1976, on the auspicious Vasant Panchami (the first day of spring, which always felt special). My mother Gita is a writer and business historian, and my father Dilip a businessman. Radhika, my younger sister, is my twin soul, if not an actual twin; we are very close. She and I studied at the J.B. Petit High School for Girls from kindergarten until my tenth-grade board examinations in 1992. J.B. Petit was selected by my mother and is, by far, the institution that has had the biggest impact on my life.

The iconic Shirin Darasha, an inspiring and path-breaking headmistress who passed away in 2012, led the school for over three decades, educating generations of girls who became independent, purposeful, compassionate (and often quirky) feminists. J.B. was affectionately known as the 'Junglee Baccha Petit School' for its many fun and whacky moments. Dress-as-you-like Fridays, when we got to exchange our blue and white chequered school uniforms for our 'home clothes', was one such idiosyncrasy.

Ms Darasha's emphasis on creativity, particularly through literature and theatre, was unparalleled in the city.

She taught us the lines from the hymn at the beginning of this book; powerful words on courage that have stayed with me over three decades later.

In eighth grade, we studied an autobiographical work by Gerald Durrell, titled *My Family and Other Animals*. It began with a defining quote by the English poet John Dryden: 'There is a pleasure sure in being mad, which none but madmen know.'[1] The quote immediately—and instinctively—became a personal motto, also making it to the front of this book.

'I remember you as a very calm, but vibrant, enthusiastic child, very bubbly, but never wild. Instead of two antennas, you had four antennas, seeking out ways to learn,' says my middle-school English teacher, Urmila Ramakrishna, who taught us the Durrell book. She was one of the earliest sponsors of my writing endeavours.

As a child I juxtaposed quiet pursuits with 'safe thrills', defined as regular spurts of adventure and excitement. Reading and writing were favourite activities, as well as stamp collecting, writing letters to pen pals, making endless lists of books read and movies watched, and playing board games.

But my childhood passion was horse-riding along with my sister and cousins. It was a sport I was introduced to by my uncle, Ajay Chacha. We trotted in the paddock, galloped on the racetrack and occasionally landed face down in sand, but most times got back on the horse immediately after a fall. My proudest moment was in 1990, when the Junior National Equestrian Championships were held in Mumbai. A teenage novice showjumper, I rode powerful horses and cleared what appeared to be intimidatingly high fences, riding with a tight stomach and seemingly calm nerves. One never knew when a horse would swerve from a fence in a last-moment refusal, leaving its rider dangling. Yet I rode because I loved it.

● ● ●

Summer 1997, Brasenose College, University of Oxford

'Who would like to volunteer?' asks the knife-thrower.
It is the annual end-of-year college ball, a night-long party that is as much part of university tradition as its historic libraries. This year the ball is circus-themed and Brasenose students are ready to celebrate. I have just finished a three-year undergraduate course in politics, philosophy and economics, and am looking forward to the ball. After all, the strenuous final examinations are over.
Now, in the middle of the night, I am taking a break from dancing and am seated in the college dining hall with friends when a professional knife-thrower asks for a volunteer to face his daggers. The daggers would put a set of kitchen knives to shame.
One of my friends raises my arm. 'Aparna would like to do it!'
I turn to him and say, 'Are you crazy?'
He says, 'Go on, I know you can.'
The knife-thrower is a professional. All I need to do is stay still, I think to myself as I walk up to the target and position myself in the allotted spot. I am wearing a lime-green kurta, last worn at my cousin's wedding six months ago. I wrap it tightly around me, making sure that none of the fabric is sticking out. I thank God for the UK's National Health Service, hold my breath and wait. The spacious, wood-panelled dining hall, normally lined with dozens of chattering students, is equally silent.
A few seconds later, there is loud applause. The daggers were accurate and I was unflinching. My friends are very proud of me.

Crazy? Impulsive? Risky? I think this incident illustrates something more nuanced—my ability to stay calm and collected when needed, while pursuing 'safe thrills'.

Oxford is known for its weekly 'essay crises', where students often stay up all night trying to complete their assignments. Final examinations at Oxford are known for their rigour. Despite these stressors, I was able to maintain my composure during the three-year undergraduate programme. A close circle of friends, a serious college relationship, lack of interpersonal conflict and a genuine interest in my chosen subjects were cornerstones of my emotional and mental equilibrium. The college relationship in particular was transformational on all counts; a wonderful way to grow and flourish as a young adult.

When it ended, a year after we left college, I could not sleep properly for days and I could not stop talking. It was obvious that I was not fully myself, with many racing and conflicting thoughts and emotions running through my head. Break-ups are significant life events for any young person. So perhaps it made sense to view my reaction, while out of character, as part of growing up and not a mental health issue. In other words, there was little to suggest then of the highs and lows to come—until the summer of 2000, before going to the Harvard Business School (HBS).

I was twenty-four then and had been working in sales and marketing with VIP luggage for three years. Midway through the year, I was accepted into HBS. The programme started in September. In the interim, I planned to take time off from the business to pursue a different sort of adventure: to intern with Randeep Sudan, a senior bureaucrat in the Andhra Pradesh government at the time. Mr Sudan worked closely with N. Chandrababu Naidu, then the chief minister of one of India's most technologically progressive states. The internship was facilitated by a family friend and I was keen on learning about state-level governance, a completely unfamiliar subject.

Come July 2000, I found myself in Hyderabad, then the capital of Andhra Pradesh, staying as a paying guest in the home of Lakshmi Devi Raj. Over the next four weeks, I acquired two role models—my innovative and approachable boss, Mr Sudan, and my host, the sixty-eight-year-old joyful and independent Lakshmi Aunty. During the day, Mr Sudan ensured I worked on stimulating projects, such as how the state could attract more external investment.

At night, Lakshmi Aunty took me on a cultural and gastronomic tour of Hyderabad's unique attraction: its larger-than-life parties. Musical evenings went on all night—I could not keep up with Lakshmi Aunty and her friends.

So it was a successful internship on all counts. My work was appreciated, so much so that Mr Sudan arranged for me to make a presentation to the chief minister and a large team at the end of my four-week internship. And two decades later, Lakshmi Aunty continues to remain a sprightly role model and a friend.

Yet inside, there was turmoil. I was consumed with anxiety and insecurity about my parents' deteriorating marriage. By then it was clear there was a major estrangement, something that I had trouble accepting. I was also deeply unhappy about another relationship break-up; someone I had been seeing for nearly two years. And I was riveted by excitement about the success of my internship.

These emotions triggered the perfect storm.

My mounting excitement—the internship, Harvard—and my raw insecurities made me impetuous, restless and hypomanic. With all the idealism of a twenty-four-year-old, I was convinced I could change the world. Blurry as the past can be, I can still remember some of the half-baked thoughts and ideas that overtook my mind in the weeks before I was due to leave for Boston. I knew I could catalyse an omnipotent coalition of Indian companies and the government to rule global markets in the prevailing dotcom era, and started drawing up grandiose plans, scribbling away on bits of paper.

Sleep disappeared as I felt invincible, restless and impetuous, going to bed late and rising early.

Kay Redfield Jamison, a renowned psychotherapist, bipolar patient and author of the classic *An Unquiet Mind*, says it best in her memoir. 'My mind was beginning to have to scramble a bit to keep up with itself, as ideas were coming so fast that they intersected one another at every inconceivable angle. There was a neuronal pileup on the highways of my brain, and the more I tried to slow down my thinking the more I became aware that I couldn't.'[2]

My family was shocked at my behavioural change. 'I know you so well. I've grown up with you. We shared a room for years. So to watch your face change, your eyes change, your mind change, in front of my eyes, was a terrifying experience. You behaved your whole life one way and then suddenly you started behaving another way, and you maintained that the new way is the real you, but Mom and I were saying, "No, something's wrong, something's different". But you were holding on to your mood as the authentic truth. It created a friction like no other. Because we were saying something's wrong. And you were saying nothing is wrong. That was the biggest clash. We didn't know what it was, we were totally in the dark,' recalls my sister Radhika.

Welcome to bipolarity.

Even though we did not acknowledge it as such at the time, it was clear by August that my thoughts, my emotions—and crucially, my sleep—were completely out of control. It was also obvious that I could not travel on my own, and my mother and sister accompanied me to Boston. We arrived at immigration only to find that my hypomanic mind had left a crucial piece of official documentation at home. It was like showing up for the Cricket World Cup without the match tickets! Luckily, the immigration officer allowed me into the country without it.

Eventually my racing thoughts subsided, I settled into my dorm room, made it to my classes and forged some sort of routine. Mom and Radhika left, and the depression set in.

HBS is known for its luxurious campus and active student body. After classes, students play tennis, go running, meet in the club-style lounge or even solve the next day's cases. I did none of that. At first, I locked myself into my dorm room after classes and cried. I wept for my recently broken relationship, I wept for my parents' fading marriage, I wept for the aching feeling of loss inside me. Later, I stopped crying, stared at the ceiling and listened to Sting's 'Ghost Story' on repeat (I liked its line 'What did not kill me just made me tougher'. It was my mantra at the time. I know there's a backlash against that line now, but back then I drew strength from it).

The room was small, just enough to house a bed, a wardrobe and an oversized music system. It opened into a common study that I shared with a roommate, Louise, a girl from Scotland with many of the same books as me on her bookshelf, who soon became a close friend. Our desks overlooked a garden of trees, expertly maintained by HBS's legendary landscaping team. As the seasons changed, the New England autumn nourished me with its magic, drawing me outdoors. I went for hikes and short road trips to see the fall colours, enjoyed a river rafting trip with my classmates. Eventually, I became more engaged with school academics and activities and found a group of classmates who also turned into lifelong friends. I began seeing a counsellor on campus, which helped to some extent.

August 2001, Mumbai

Back home for a summer break between my first and second years of business school, I am at a cousin's engagement party in our family home, wearing a light pink ghaghra that contrasts with the red-hot rebellion brewing inside me. There is dancing, music, poetry and dinner, but my mind is swaying to a tune of its own. Negative emotions are building up inside me like expanding steam. Perhaps I am angry because my recently concluded summer internship at an investment bank has not gone well—I did not get a job offer. Perhaps I am still upset about the situation at home. Whatever the reasons, my behaviour deteriorates towards the bizarre—I am restless and impulsive. My mother, sister and I retreat to a family member's beach house to try and calm me down, where I stay up all night talking to myself. When my father asks me later, 'What goes through your mind at these times?', I say—'It's like there's a script, and I need to act on it.' Over a few days, my equilibrium is restored, and I make it back to business school just in time for the start of the second year.

In my second year, I lived off-campus, in a house with three girls. We were close friends but there were times when the melancholy would re-emerge, often prompted by loneliness. I remember a quiet weekend when everyone was out. I looked out of the kitchen window, held a knife to my wrist and thought—this is all it would take. But then I reminded myself that 'this' would take for ever for me to bleed to death. Instead, I came across *Moth Smoke* on my bookshelf, a novel by British-Pakistani author Mohsin Hamid, which captivated me for the rest of the weekend. So much so that I later told a close friend and classmate, 'It was the worst weekend of my life, but then it turned out to be one of the best.'

Personalized projects made me happier. I realized I enjoyed research-led field studies rather than conventional classes and pursued these options as much as possible. Supervised by individual professors and done either singly or in groups of two and three students, field studies allowed me to collaborate with my friends and get closer to them whilst exploring my research interests. I also signed up for a life-changing creative writing class with the Harvard undergraduates, across the Charles River, held every week in a small room with a large square table and stained-glass windows, and became more regular at yoga. In the end, the depression wore off naturally, without medication, and I graduated without incident, with my classmates.

Since then, nearly every year or every other year, there has been what we in the family refer to as a 'manic episode': about a dozen in twenty years, with varying degrees of amplitude and frequency, interspersed with some periods of depression and long stretches of 'normality'—which include minor oscillations on a daily basis.

What is bipolarity? Also known as manic depression, it is characterized by extreme shifts in mood and energy levels due to certain triggers that cause chemical reactions in the brain. In my experience, these emotions are like the ups and downs that any of us experience in a normal day, but much more intense, such that they are completely ungovernable. As the American Psychiatric Association (APA) says, 'People with bipolar disorder experience intense emotional states that typically occur during distinct periods of days to weeks, called mood episodes. These mood episodes are categorized as manic/hypomanic (abnormally happy or irritable mood) or depressive (sad mood).'[3]

Bipolarity comes in different shapes and sizes, based on the type of mood swings. Bipolar I disorder, which has the most severe mood swings and is what I live with, has mania as a defining feature. It is probably the aspect of bipolarity that is hardest to explain yet provokes the most curiosity— and concern—amongst others. The characteristics of a manic episode are easy to identify—and relatable, in my case.

According to the APA,[4] 'A manic episode is a period of at least one week when a person is extremely high-spirited or irritable most of the day for most days, possesses more energy than usual, and experiences at least three of the following changes in behavior':

o   Decreased need for sleep (e.g., feeling energetic despite significantly less sleep than usual)
o   Increased or faster speech
o   Uncontrollable racing thoughts or quickly changing ideas or topics when speaking
o   Distractibility
o   Increased activity (e.g., restlessness, working on several projects at once)
o   Increased risky behavior (e.g., reckless driving, spending sprees).[5]

It is important to distinguish mania from hypomania, which the APA says is 'characterized by less severe manic symptoms that need to last only four days in a row rather than a week. Hypomanic symptoms do not lead to the major problems in daily functioning that manic symptoms commonly cause.'[6] In my experience, mania is more intense and less frequent, while hypomania is milder but can lurk around the corner and requires even more vigilance (In the book, I have referred to hypomania and mania almost interchangeably as there were some incidents when I was sure I was manic and others where my memory is less precise). The neuroscience of bipolarity is still not very well understood, but what is known is that it is highly heritable and that it is a brain disorder due to chemical imbalances in the brain.

'People with bipolar disorder generally have periods of neutral mood as well. When treated, people with bipolar disorder can lead full and productive lives,' says the APA.[7] I would strongly echo that. Bipolarity is a continuum and the extremes of mania happen less than 10 per cent of the time in my case. Most days, I am 'normal' but I can swerve towards hypomania or depression in a matter of days and must remain self-aware.

About 0.6 per cent of the Indian population is bipolar,[8] concludes 'The Burden of Mental Disorders Across the States of India: The Global Burden of Disease Study 1990–2017' in the *Lancet Psychiatry* journal, one of the most important studies of mental health in India. It found that 'one in seven Indians were affected by mental disorders of varying severity in 2017. . . In 2017 alone, 197.3 million people had mental disorders in India',[9] more than the rates of cancer prevalence.[10] THIS IS HUGE. The majority of patients are untreated, stigmatized and suffering.

Let's think about it. All of us know some friend or family member trying to cope with such a mental health condition, to varying degrees of success. Yet it is vital to note that even a serious mental health illness such as bipolarity is not a lifelong disability. But as many as 59 per cent to 63 per cent of individuals with bipolar disorder were affected by disability in multiple domains, mainly pertaining to 'work, social and family life',[11] says the 'National Mental Health Survey of India, 2015–16: Prevalence, Patterns and Outcomes', another landmark report on mental health in India, published by the National Institute of Mental Health and Neurosciences (NIMHANS).

Mental health conditions now cause one in five years lived with disability,[12] with individuals not living to their full potential. These are alarming statistics—and only exacerbated by Covid-19, which is said to have 'disrupted mental health services in 93% of countries'[13] according to the World Economic Forum.

We did not know any of this when I graduated from business school in 2002. My mother and sister watched the rained-out graduation ceremony on campus, we had a family barbeque with my housemates before we said our farewells, followed by a trip to the Grand Canyon, Las Vegas and Los Angeles with my father and sister.

A few months later, I was back in the family business—now elevated to the head of sales and marketing of Blow Plast Ergonomics (as it was then called), our family's modular office furniture business. It had suffered losses after the dotcom bust and my father wanted my help to turn it around. I did not know the difference between a panel system and a desk but I threw myself into absorbing it all, with regular trips to architects and designers, to ongoing fit-out sites, to customers across the country and to our factories in Nagpur. I soon took over the business as its head and it was to become one of the most defining experiences of my life.

Yet I ran into a hiccup, another bout of hypomania in 2003, which nearly led to my exit from the business (which I will discuss in more detail in later chapters). I recovered and so did the business. By 2004 it was profitable, fast-growing, and I was enjoying running it.

Enter Amit.

Towards the end of 2003, I received an email that intrigued me. It was from one Amit Raje, who said he wanted to apply to HBS and had got my contact details from a common friend. The friend was an older HBS alum, who suggested that Amit connect with me as I was a recent graduate and involved with the alumni club at the time. Amit's email recounted a dramatic story of self-made progress from humble beginnings in Mumbai to work experience in Delhi's 'corridors of power' and a nascent career in a financial services company in Mumbai. Drama extended to his personal life too—he had survived a perilous fall from a moving local train. Amit's father Avinash was a retired shop floor supervisor, his mother Asha a primarily Marathi-speaking, former telephone operator-turned-homemaker and Amit aspired to study at Harvard. It did sound fascinating.

But our first meeting, at my Worli home, was anything but promising. I was mildly hungover after an excessive Saturday night; he was hungry and all I served him was a shared apple (he often reminds me). For my part, I thought he had a terrible haircut and wore a shirt that made him look like a jailbird. His essays would have to be completely rewritten too, I said, which I wasn't about to do. He did not get into his choice of business school and decided to stay in Mumbai and reapply the following year.

Which meant, of course, that we were able to get to know each other a bit better and we began to speak quite regularly. I learnt that he could recite the dialogues of the Hollywood blockbuster *Gladiator* and the Marathi political drama *Sinhasan* with equal ease. That he was a former competitive bowler who had played with Sachin Tendulkar as a teenager. And one year later, in September 2004, when he showed up on Ganesh Chaturthi in a smart white kurta to discuss his essays again, I quickly re-evaluated my opinion of his overall presentability! We started dating and it soon became clear that this was serious. How to share the news with my parents was less obvious. The socio-economic gap between us was enormous. 'My entire house can fit into your living room,' said Amit, describing his compact home in the suburbs. His bank balance and salary were modest at best. He didn't own a car or even know how to drive.

But he had got into the London Business School and I knew the MBA would be an equalizer, that he would be offered opportunities to propel him upwards and forwards. I was attracted by his determination, perseverance and ambition, the undiluted adventure that he represented, so different from my contemporaries. I just had to persuade my parents and my extended family to see it my way.

Luckily, ill-health intervened. I contracted hepatitis in December 2004 and was housebound. Amit visited me regularly after work, taking the last train home from the closest train station in Dadar. My mother witnessed our growing bond, which helped lessen her anxiety to some extent. The deciding factor was his very respected mentor, a prominent individual with whom he had worked in Delhi, who met my parents and spoke for him, reassuring them about his future prospects. My father also came around, eventually.

Nine months later, in June 2005, we were married. The preceding weeks had been full of music and masti—my friends, family and I had a hugely entertaining dance teacher for the sangeet preparation. He kept us on our toes and had us in splits. The traditional mehendi, sangeet, wedding ceremony and reception were accompanied by a Venetian-style masquerade, where, for once, I loved dressing up and dancing in a custom-designed, floor-length ball gown. Some friends from abroad flew down, which was very special. It was a perfect weekend in every way; I was a fortunate bride who got to enjoy her wedding; my family noticed that I remained calm and poised during a major moment of transition.

May 2006, London

It is a lovely evening, nearly a year after our wedding. I am taking the underground train back home after finishing a day's work at an advertising agency. I get off one station before my stop and walk over to the London Business School, where Amit is studying for his MBA. We walk home and have dinner together. It is a simple meal, home-cooked and microwaved, and we watch TV—movies, the news—or just chat.

We moved to London immediately after our wedding and our time there can only be described as an extended two-year honeymoon. It felt like an uncomplicated and happy existence, and I was mentally and emotionally stable for over three years, starting from mid-2003 to the end of 2006. Since Amit was studying, I found a job, as a strategist and creative planner in an advertising agency, to support us. I was still involved with the office furniture business in some ways but as it didn't have any operations in London, it did not constitute full-time paid employment.

My working hours were more than reasonable, allowing Amit and I to spend a lot of time with each other. We were careful with money, saving as much as we could to pay off his student loan, but we met friends regularly, went to the cinema, had a few short bed-and-breakfast-type holidays and treated ourselves to the occasional restaurant. My maternal grandfather Sohanlal, my uncle Mukesh and my aunt Ruchi lived upstairs from us, and we often had Sunday lunches with them.

I still do not know what triggered it, the next time it happened. One moment I was on holiday in Mumbai during the winter of December 2006 and January 2007, and the next thing I knew my mind was manufacturing disturbed thoughts, including a delusion that my sister was at risk of physical harm. Perhaps I was stressed about work (I was reinvolved in the family business for those weeks), perhaps I was trying to do too much (I was commuting between Amit's home and my mother's place), perhaps I had too many social commitments (a friend was having a big wedding), perhaps there were unresolved feelings about my father's remarriage. Whatever it was, I imploded. I was so anxious about my sister that I told my family I needed to see her immediately. She was working in New York at the time and I flew there to spend a few days with her. Of course, she freed me from my anxiety, saying she was fine and had always been.

She also had to manage me alone in her apartment. Radhika recalls, 'In that trip, you asked me, "Can I go for a walk?" I had to go to work, and I said, "Yes, I understand. You can go for a walk." That day, I was truly worried because it meant you were just walking around New York City by yourself. What if you didn't come back? That would be my responsibility. But I took a leap of faith because you asked me, I trusted you enough. Who can stay in an apartment all day, those were pre-Covid times? And I also thought it's not my role to give Aparna permission. I've always felt that. It's not my role to give her permission. She's her own person who has to give herself permission.'

That morning, I walked into a hotel, sat there for hours having a cup of tea and wrote a poem. Then I flew home to London and gave Amit the tightest hug I could. I was back.

A few months later, on Father's Day in June 2007, we discovered I was pregnant. Amit's MBA programme was also ending and we decided to come back home to Mumbai. It was a moment of flux—we did not have a home or an income and had a baby on the way. I often reflected on our tenuous future, sitting in the bus on the way home from work in London in the months leading to our return, but it did not stress me. And it worked out. We found a charming two-bedroom rental by the sea in Mahim, Amit found a job in a private equity firm, leaving me to concentrate on prenatal yoga, prenatal classes and prenatal baby reading.

Thanks to all the yoga, baby Amartya came into the world easily enough in February 2008. But nothing—not the books, not the classes, not the BabyCentre emails—prepared me for breastfeeding. My new nanny, Champadevi Paswan, and I did not get along at first, and I was suspicious of her child-rearing methods. I was unable to sleep at night because of the night feeds and I could not rest in the day when Amartya slept.

Postpartum depression is a common enough phenomenon but this was not depression—my mind was pushing me into unwanted territory. Horrific nightmares of sexual violence took over, driving me over the edge for the first couple of weeks. But I continued to nurse Amartya. He has always been a caring, mature and empathetic child, and I often wonder if that is because, somehow, he intuited, even as an infant, what his mother went through to nurse him, initially.

November 2008, Mumbai

Unusually, I have the TV on in the morning in the living room. There's a special reason—president-elect Barack Obama is making a historic victory speech in Chicago. Giving me company is baby Amartya, then eight months old. A blanket has been laid out with his toys, as it is every morning. Later, he will sleep and I will work on my articles. In the evening, he will be taken in his stroller to Shivaji Park and I will go for a walk to my favourite public park next door.

After the storm of the first two weeks receded and the 'nightmares' vanished, I was able to enjoy being a new mother, a phase that lasted an uninterrupted four years. For the first time since leaving university, I was not working full-time. Instead, I took a year off to nurse Amartya and pursue my hobbies—I had always enjoyed writing (an inherited gene from my mother), and my first column in the *Mint* newspaper was published when Amartya was six months old. I also did a short English literature course with my former English teacher Helen Mathur, briefly led a women's network and played a lot with my baby—we read books, played with toys, went on play dates, travelled and began attending a local mother–toddler programme together.

By the time he was two years old, my first article in the UK's *Financial Times Weekend* was published and I was an established freelancer. The year off from corporate life turned into three years and in December 2010, Agastya was born. This time, I was prepared. Despite Amit's pronounced anxiety about the birth, neither breastfeeding nor sleep deprivation were a problem. Once again, I nursed Agastya for as long as I could and spent my days with both boys. It was an idyllic time—I was a mother of two generally easy-going young kids, with an evolving, flexible work-from-home writing career, and a (now) supportive and trusted nanny.

January 2012, a factory outside Chandigarh

My colleague and I are travelling to the family's office furniture factory outside Chandigarh. Thoughts are buzzing in my head like irritating bees, so much so that I need to rush to the privacy of my hotel room and spit them out into my voice recorder before I even make it to the factory. I am back in the family business, looking after marketing and trying to turn it around. My mother is keen on selling the business and a family friend and adviser wanted my help to improve its valuation for the sale. But the landscape has completely altered since my previous tenure. My former colleagues have left, margins have dwindled and the world has had an economic meltdown. I am trying to combine family life with a toddler and an infant, freelance writing and a business turnaround. It is a lot to take on and sleep slips away. So my mind responds in the only way it knows—it rebels.

I remember this manic episode vividly. Mania ascended with frightening familiarity. The physical symptoms were immediate indicators—a wired body, struggling to sleep for more than a few hours and the constant adrenaline. It is always physically gruelling. And that's when the words and thoughts started emerging, first like butterflies released from a net, light and delicate, but ending up like a dagger plunged into one's back, brutal, bloodied and relentless.

Initially, a sense of euphoria 'connected' me to the universe. There was a feeling of being 'alive' like no other. A grand scheme was floated to change the world, where I was the driving catalyst. It rapidly gained momentum. Poems, bits of screenplays, prose pieces and voice notes, expressions of my far-reaching ambitions, slid out of me. But then another insidious form of paranoia dominated—scenes of sexual trauma. Themes of incest and sexual torture held me mentally hostage. I became delusional, imagining that these awful acts were actually happening, to people I knew, by people I knew. The reasons for these are complicated and not entirely clear to me (I have never been sexually abused myself). Regardless of their origins, they haunted me.

The mind became the minefield.

My family held an urgent conclave. 'Mom, Amit and I had a conversation about your career. And we decided, rightly or wrongly, that being a CEO was too stressful for you, that business stress seemed to trigger these episodes and that we all felt sad about that decision. But we would be united,' says Radhika. I didn't know about the conversation but I do remember my mother asking me not to run the business and my disappointment at that outcome. I had no choice though. I had to accept the decision.

This was also the time I started writing a journal. Once I had calmed down, in May 2012, I reflected:

I have to acknowledge that I had trouble managing my emotions during a period of transition for all of us, because of some important underlying issues, including my sense of identity & my ambitions for myself:

I cannot deny that coming back to Ergo felt like a homecoming, in many ways. The positive reaction from customers, architects, employees and competitors was gratifying, especially since I was away for such a long time. Friends and acquaintances from outside the industry seemed to endorse the sentiment that I was doing the right thing, for myself, and my family. Even though I was clear that I did not want to tie myself to an asset or consider Ergo "mine" in anyway, at some point, the desire to try and "fix" it overtook me, resulting in a gap between expectations and reality.

The yin and yang pairing of mania and depression was evident as I wrote in my journal in July 2012:

Agastya's first day at mother–toddler at [the preschool] Rishikul, and while it was momentous in its own way—he was so thrilled to go out and wear new shoes—it was also tinged with a little disappointment. My time with Amartya seems like a different world, less troubled, more innocent. I was happy then, not suffering from existentialist angst as much as I am now! I have to acknowledge that I'm feeling a little lonely now.

The incident was just one of many where I grappled with identity issues, a subject which I will discuss at length in chapter eight on self-therapy. In any case, the company was sold soon after, in August 2012. I got back to journalism, lining up some exciting projects, expanding my writing beyond the workplace, to cities and urbanization. By the end of the year, I was a lot happier, having spent more time with the children and having been on rejuvenating family holidays to Singapore and Coorg.

⚫ ⚫ ⚫

What does mania feel like? Every bipolar person's experience of mania will be different, given individual personalities, but perhaps the process of what governs it may not be so varied.

To me, mania is a tornado. It is an illusion. It is misguided energy. It is imagination at its best—and worst. And it is visceral.

Let me explain all five aspects.

First, as a doctor illustrated to me with a compelling metaphor, bipolar people get sucked into tornadoes when stressed, excited or conflicted in any way. While others might collapse with too many deadlines or commitments, bipolar people get caught up in a tornado that takes them higher and higher, disconnected from solid ground. Ultimately, the tornado rises so high that one ends up hallucinating. This is mania.

The second way I look at mania is that it is an illusion. It draws on my deepest susceptibilities—ambition, insecurities, fears, ego—to convince me that *this is who I am. This is a better me.* It is maya at its most convincing and it gives me permission to do things I wouldn't normally do, to act on impulse or suspend judgement.

Studies show that bipolar people have a propensity to veer towards excess, whether alcohol, drugs or outbursts on social media. 'Patients with bipolar I and II disorder have an extremely high rate of co-occurring substance use disorders', with bipolar I patients having a '40% lifetime prevalence of alcohol and other drug use disorders' says a paper titled 'The Prevalence and Significance of Substance Use Disorders in Bipolar Type I and II Disorder'.[14] There is less academic research on the link between bipolarity and social media but plenty of anecdotal evidence. Shreevatsa Nevatia, a journalist and the bipolar protagonist of one of my favourite mental health memoirs, *How to Travel Light: My Memories of Madness and Melancholia*, devotes an entire chapter to his escapades on Facebook during his highs and lows.[15]

My preferred sin is writing. I often come across scraps of paper lying around the house, tucked away at the top of a filing cabinet or at the back of a bathroom drawer, and I cringe. I don't need to read the intense handwritten scribbles, with words veering in all directions, connected with circles and lines, to glean my state of mind when I wrote it. Remember the scene in the 2001 film, *A Beautiful Mind*, when Alicia Nash walks into her paranoid schizophrenic husband's office to witness a hurricane of confusion? Random newspaper clippings are papered all over the room's wall, lacking coherence or structure. She is horrified to see the extent of his madness. That's how I feel when I confront myself with the evidence of my own insanity. This is mania.

Third, sudden spurts in intellectual and emotional energy. When I go back and look at the few bits of remaining evidence from my manic episodes—most of my writing I destroy as soon as I recover—what strikes me is just how energized I was during those moments. So much passion, so much intensity and so much creativity animate my voice and my outlook. The urgency of these energies can be frightening to family members. As my mind races, the slower pace of actual family life becomes frustrating.

Sometimes though, when I feel sluggish and heavy on a 'regular' day, I envy my manic firepower. The question is—is mania the right expression of these energies? And the answer, of course, is no. That is one of the reasons why this book is so important to me—because it is a socially acceptable expression of these energies.

Fourth, mania's other weapon is imagination, which creates a dream-like reality that is exciting, entertaining and just plain fun. As one of my doctors told me, 'When you're manic, you look for excitement in places where you know it can be found.'

Imagination makes you feel alive, like nothing else. I love these lines from *Hurry Down Sunshine: A Father's Memoir of Love and Madness*, by journalist Michael Greenberg, about his daughter, Sally Greenberg, the fifteen-year-old bipolar protagonist of the book. 'Everything fell into place,' Sally says. 'I don't know how to describe it. My mind was going incredibly fast. But time slowed. I could see underneath the surface of things. I could see inside people. It was like I had been sleepwalking until then, waiting for this to happen.'[16]

But imagination can also have frightening, damaging consequences, such as hallucinations and delusions. It is a destructive seduction of one's emotions at its most lethal because it convinces a manic person that their emotions are legitimate and their actions are sound. When there is an orchestral universe inside my head, it is hard not to pay full attention to its grandeur. This is mania.

Finally, mania is visceral. Bipolar disorder is generally regarded as a mental, emotional and behavioural health issue. In my experience, its effect on the body adds an additional layer of complexity.

I judge the intensity of any emotion commonly associated with mania or hypomania—whether anger, aggression or excitement—through my body. If I am experiencing any emotion that may lead to a manic episode, my body is the first to warn me.

My breath is shorter and shallower, my back is tightened, my hand less steady, my brain is foggy, my sleep is disturbed and, most of all, my gut is exploding. It is on *fire*, a *visceral* feeling in a way like nothing else. This is primeval, and because it is *my very own body* that is combustible, it is hard not to be seduced by these emotions, to deny that this is truly *me*, that these emotions are real, they are meaningful and that I must act on them.

Why do emotions scatter themselves all over the body? My intuitive conclusion is that this is the result of heart, head and hand not being aligned with each other; it is an expression of inner conflict. When the heart and head disagree, the hand has no choice but to get in the way and the body reacts. This, then, is mania.

But back in 2012, we still didn't have a word for it.

For that, I would have to wait for Bihar.

After nearly two weeks of medication, I have to say I'm feeling better. A few weeks of irrational, manic behaviour (again) all I can say is a feeling of thanks, to those who love me.

I'm finally ready to acknowledge that this is a medical condition, and that it needs medical treatment. I'm reassured by the shrink we have, Dr Gaurav Sharma [name changed]—it makes all the difference. Conversations with [friends and medical professionals] Shama and Roop Majli about lithium, the pill I've been prescribed, have also been hugely comforting.

27 February 2013

This is a low phase: I'm feeling really disappointed with myself, worried about the future and embarrassed about my past indiscretions. When will this narrative end? At the moment, all I'm determined to do is to ensure that there are no more episodes in the next five years. I'm frustrated that with just the slightest bit of success or stress, my mind goes off on a tangent: it's deeply distressing, actually. Anyway, I need to get some work done, rather than dwelling on acts that I cannot change.

4 March 2013
(extracts from journals)

2

Me vs Me
(2013–2018)

After I returned from Bihar, Dr Raman Deshpande, one of India's best-known onco surgeons, and a mentor to Amit, introduced us to Dr Sharma, a seasoned psychiatrist. With a discreet clinic in south Mumbai, I felt in safe hands with Dr Sharma (I will write about getting on medication in more detail in the chapter on medical therapies).

Towards the end of the year, in November, I wrote this poem:

Turning Point

There are no headlines today
No cocktail launch parties, or awards ceremonies
No business-class seats and frequent-flier miles

There is the private knowledge,
That today was a day
Where nothing was written
Which would later be regretted.

That today was a day
Where it didn't occur to me

How easy it would be to jump off a building.
Today, I didn't have to dismiss the thought.

Today, there's a London bus made out of a cardboard box.
There is camping under a blanket
Strung between two wooden dining chairs, in the living room.

Today, there are
No moments of despair
No delusions of grandeur

Instead, an attitude of gratitude
Moments of simplicity and spontaneity
And the promise of purpose.

One of my favourite poems, I wrote 'Turning Point' to mark a personal milestone: after several weeks of struggling with depression and waking up every day to a sense of hopelessness, I finally managed to rid myself of suicidal thoughts. Of course, I sat at the edge of my bed and cried but I also felt much better after writing it.

I have never actually harmed myself or made any attempt to do so, but there was a distinct period of my life, for a large part of 2013, during which I was confronted by a large, bleak void every morning. Life seemed just—empty.

Given that my manic episode at the ashram was one of my most lethal, it was little surprise that I had to contend with depression for as long as I did. I knew I could get on to additional medication to elevate my spirits—and there were several sleepless nights when I nearly called Dr Sharma and asked him to do so—but Amit and I were committed to finding a solution without additional medication, and we did.

I didn't lie around on the sofa or in my bedroom—my days were fairly busy with work and family commitments. There were interviews to be conducted and copies to be filed. My colleagues were friendly and stimulating.

Home life was also a pillar. Our apartment in Mahim had a rare view of the Arabian Sea and of one of Mumbai's nicest public parks, a hidden gem called Dhote Udyan. The rhythm of the waves and the canopy of greenery outside my windows were enough to lift any melancholy spirits. But I felt unhappy and vacant. I couldn't find joy or happiness in anything around me.

And in a city full of skyscrapers, jumping off one of them seemed preferable to wrestling with this inner black hole every day. I remember, at one point, mentally comparing the available building options to see which one seemed the most viable, my parents' home or mine. Once I even made it to my building's terrace before turning back, scowling at myself for even having come this far. I rejected the option every time it crossed my mind because I knew I didn't want to be defeated by my illness.

Any well-intentioned onlooker would have urged me to consider my obligations to my family and to desist from this line of thought. It is not that I was ready to abandon my family. It was just that my self-esteem was so low during those months that I honestly didn't think it would make a big difference to anyone in the long run if I wasn't around any more. I really felt they wouldn't notice my absence or it wouldn't matter—when the truth is, of course, that they would have been devastated. Depressed and despairing, my duties to my family were not motivating factors at all. Perhaps I am not alone in making this admission.

In fact, it was the other way around—it was my family who helped me overcome my black hole, even though they may not have gauged its true depths. I think I was quite good at concealing it. As I will explain in more detail a little bit later, they helped me see the daily joys of simple family life.

But it took several months before I could rid myself fully of semi-suicidal notions, as can be seen from the timing of the poem. Luckily, they haven't returned; a fact I know my family and friends will be most relieved to hear.

Slowly, over the course of a few months, I left the black hole behind. And then one day in November, I found myself writing this poem to celebrate the fact that I had, actually, much to celebrate in life and even more to look forward to. As the first paragraph suggests, I was also finally ready to shed my preoccupation with all the markers of a successful business life—the seemingly glittery lifestyle, the award ceremonies and the hoopla. Something just as meaningful, if not more, was waiting to be discovered.

My end-of-year diary captured the many highlights of 2013 (I am sharing in some detail to show how multifaceted life can be and how full of simple pleasures):

Travels with family—peacocks and baby goats in [our hometown] Bagar in Rajasthan, parks in London, museums in Austria, adventure sports in Munnar. Family brunches at Mom's. Speaking at the SIX conference at Seoul. Agastya starts preschool on his own. Amartya plays the drum twice in front of an audience. Amu wins a school art competition. Making stuff at home: cardboard buses, trains, paintings. Vivarea, planning our first permanent home. Nature walks in Borivali national park. Play dates with moms at home and elsewhere. Girls' night outs. Anchor on pilot CNBC Awaaz TV show. *Mint* and *FT* stories continue with some interesting profiles. Started reading again as part of Mary's book club. Spent many nights watching movies with Amit at home and at Phoenix Mills. Most important: recover from a serious, prolonged manic-depressive episode.

Some writers reserve their works for themselves, but I like feedback (preferably instantaneously). I needed to share

'Turning Point' with someone, and I knew my family might get alarmed with the poem's implications, so I turned to a trusted childhood friend, Sandhini, an art curator, and emailed her the poem, saying:

> Hello madame,
>
> Here's another piece I wrote about coming to terms with my condition. Since this stuff is so personal, I can't really share with family—they might really freak out about some of it. For me, I need to write and then to share with someone: and you seem to be on the receiving end of my bipolar-inspired poetry!
>
> I'm optimistic about moving in the right direction. Would like to chat whenever you have time—it's not urgent. Let me know what you think.
>
> Lots of love,
> Aparna

She wrote back:

> Thank you for trusting me with this, I feel very touched and humbled. Love you lots—so looking forward to coming home on the 26th.
> Hang in there, you're a fabulous person.

To which I replied:

> Thanks for your understanding, I knew I could count on you to read the layers without getting too agitated. Have a good trip, and see you when you're back.

My friend's reply was perfect—empathetic and non-judgemental. Her intuitive understanding of my state of mind and appropriate choice of words helped lift me out of my black hole. It was a ray of light, to be able to share my writing with a friend who was willing to receive and interpret it for what it was and not ascribe a layer of judgement to it.

My friend later told me that the poem did, in fact, worry her when she first read it, but she realized that my writing was 'a conversation Aparna was having with herself' and not suicidal in its intent. As an experienced curator, I knew that she would be able to interpret and grasp the inherent optimism of the piece, and not get distracted by the sense of hopelessness in the first few lines of the poem. 'I was feeling terrible, but I'm doing much better now, and I'd like you to know that it's been a slightly challenging journey, but I'm closer to the destination'—that's what the poem said.

As a writer, I respond to my illness through writing. Sharing my poems, in particular, is how I share my emotions with my loved ones. It is a way of reaching out, letting someone know how I'm feeling. The act of sharing my thoughts and feelings, on paper, with friends and family, helps me gain some much-needed distance from them. It continues to be one of the most vital aspects of my therapy.

● ● ●

Understanding Mental Disorders: Your Guide to DSM-5 is a layperson's guide to the fifth edition of the *Diagnostic and Statistical Manual of Mental Disorders (DSM-5)*, the textbook of modern psychiatry. The DSM is sometimes dismissed these days because of the controversies in the process involved in creating it, as well as some of the outcomes it generates, but I find it to be a very useful reference. It describes the symptoms of a 'major depressive episode' in bipolar disorder as below. 'A person with a major depressive episode has at least five of the following symptoms for two weeks, has a decline from his or her normal social or work function and must have one of the first two symptoms on the list.'[1] The symptoms for someone with major depressive disorder (MDD), i.e., depressed but not suffering from bipolarity, are almost exactly the same and they include, the DSM says:

o   Depressed mood or sadness lasting most of the day, nearly every day (feels sad, empty or hopeless),
o   great loss of interest or pleasure in all or almost all activities that were once enjoyed,
o   sudden change in appetite, with weight gain or loss,
o   insomnia or hypersomnia (sleeping too little or too much),
o   feeling restless or agitated (as seen in pacing or hand-wringing) or having slowed speech and movements (behaviour must be noticed by others),
o   fatigue or loss of energy,
o   feeling worthless or guilty,
o   trouble keeping focused or making decisions,
o   and frequent thoughts of death or suicide, a suicide plan, or suicide attempt.[2]

Each of us knows someone who has suffered from or is suffering from depression. Depression is a universal, invisible and deadly parasite.

One in twenty Indians suffer from depression but the vast majority are untreated, says the NIMHANS study.[3] This is millions of people, across all walks of life—and the study was conducted well before Covid-19, which has only magnified depression and anxiety. 'Most of those identified had not sought care or when sought, was not available. Factors ranging from awareness to affordability, varying between rural and urban areas, need to be critically delineated to address specific issues in bridging treatment gap,' the report elaborates.[4]

Untreated illness has a direct impact on one's ability to be productive and happy. 'Individuals with depressive disorders and bipolar affective disorders on an average were unable to carry out their daily activities for 20 days in the previous one month,' the NIMHANS report says, underlining the gravity of the issue and advocating assessment and rehabilitation.[5] What triggers depression? To a bipolar person, depression is as inevitable as death and taxes. Or to paraphrase Shakespeare, I believe that depression must follow mania, 'as the night follows the day'. This has been my experience, at least. And as Dr Sharma told me, 'Mania is hard on the family, depression is hard on you.' I would add: it is longer-lasting and much less visible. Experts agree. 'Although mania or hypomania are the defining characteristics of bipolar disorder, people with a diagnosis tend to spend much more time depressed than manic during the course of the illness,' state Sarah Owen and Amanda Saunders, authors of *Bipolar Disorder: The Ultimate Guide*. Owen and Saunders are journalists, cousins and family members of bipolar patients.[6]

By the end of 2013, I felt much better. Three new projects kept me occupied, in addition to my writing for the *Mint* and the *FT*—planning the design of our permanent home in a gated community called Vivarea, helping my mother with some property rentals and anchoring a pilot TV show for CNBC Awaaz.

Back in early 2013, I was lucky to get a professional break when I needed it. I had been discussing a pilot TV show for some time with Sanjay Pugalia, a family friend and then editor of the Hindi business news channel CNBC

Awaaz. I shared my depressive feelings with Sanjayji, how I needed more contact with the outside world. We decided to go ahead with a show on workplaces on his channel. Attitude of gratitude, indeed a tonic for depression.

Familiar with my mental health issues, I was given enough time to complete the project. Even though the pilot didn't turn into a full-time show, I was very grateful for the opportunity. Just having my hair blow-dried regularly and figuring out which sari to wear turned into a joyful task!

The house move in early 2014 was smooth, ensuring no yo-yoing for many months, as I noted:

27 August 2014

The last few months seem to have flown by—our move into Vivarea has taken on a life of its own, with many more intellectual and social commitments. I feel like I've done little else in the last six months apart from organizing salons, dinners, play dates, festive events, house-warmings, holidays and classes for the family and myself. And of course, there's the mom part and property manager, and, somewhere in between, a columnist and journalist. It feels like I've taken six months off to refresh myself and get fitter—and it's worth it.

I'm particularly pleased that I made it through the 'danger zone' of Nov 13–March 14 [where I was managing three challenging projects, with concurrent deadlines], without having a manic episode. For a change, I took help on all three and downsized expectations and my role to help me navigate them, which seemed to have worked.

So a peaceful interlude ensued for most of 2013 and 2014, until . . .

November 2014, New Delhi

I am at a two-day conference of global urban thinkers at a hotel in New Delhi, and I am having an emotional catharsis. Downstairs, at the event, I hold stimulating and serious conversations with intellectual heavyweights, ask questions, listen and focus. Upstairs in my room, words are pouring out of me. I write poems and a letter to my mentor, which starts off at four pages and never seems to end. Once again, sleep eludes me. My friend and roommate Jessica, whom I had invited to share a room, reads what I write and witnesses my rapid retreat into a fantasy world without judging it.

'I had never spent time with somebody who was very lucid and aware of the shift in and out of multiple realities, seeing that as the other side of a lot of creativity and writing flow. That was new. You would write and sometimes your writing would take on a different character and voice when you were slipping away from being grounded in the here and now. There is a creative genius trope in history but I hadn't actually ever been sitting next to anyone who was personally kind of working through that, or surfing through it, is maybe a better word? You have this immensely powerful, creative joy in untethering, which is also potentially really destructive for you and everyone around you; you're on a knife's edge. But I could also see that you were trying to manage a level of chaos that was flowing through you in a constructive way,' she observes.

I was unable to focus on sitting through the panel discussions but I managed to pull myself together for the one-on-one interviews, though my subjects could see how tired I was. The conversations were some of the most intellectually challenging dialogues I've ever had—just an indication of the brain's productivity when hypomanic.

'I had no idea how to help. And I also knew that I couldn't really ask you directly how to help because you weren't fully able to say, "Okay, well, this is what I needed to do." So I thought, "Okay, when she's sleeping, I'm not going to disturb her",' Jessica says.

She worried about how I would make it back to Mumbai if I deteriorated, but I managed to put myself on the flight back home and promptly found myself in the doctor's clinic on my return. Sadly, I visited him regularly from November 2014 to March 2018, tackling manic or hypomanic episodes followed by weeks of lows.

There were moments when I stepped off the ride to try and reflect and document my emotions, as can be seen from this note, written after the emergence of a short burst of hypomania in August 2016. Even though it was nipped in the bud, the hypomania left behind its own sting in the tail in the form of feeling despondent (although not fully depressed).

Friday, 12 August 2016

Am really beginning to wonder if I'm forever doomed to these up and down cycles. How do I unlock myself from what can seem to be a prison of pendulums?

And again, three weeks later, a note that illustrates how feeling low can coexist with an active social life (or maybe, for some people, because of it):

Tuesday, 6 September 2016

A long and unusually social weekend; especially Saturday (two children's birthday parties, an art event, family dinner, friend's birthday celebration), then family lunch for Mom's birthday on Sunday, and then the lovely annual, house-to-house ritual of Ganpati at both [our old home] Shireesh and [current home] Vivarea, interspersed with Amartya's school revision. So much to celebrate.

But I find myself still feeling down and that *down* stems from one source—to which I still haven't found an answer, after so many years of writing this journal: purpose. Or rather, I do find purpose in my writing, but I still feel like a failure compared to all the people I know with full-time jobs & tangible achievements.

This comparison is entirely self-concocted and I know I need to be more compassionate with myself, but it's hard to find the means to do so. My earlier formula— of pursuing happiness as a goal, instead of success—is failing me on this occasion. I know I need to take myself a little less seriously, but it's hard to do so when surrounded by so many achievers in my universe.

By the end of the year, when I was a little too emotional once again, I tried to seek inner stillness and probe for insights into my condition:

Wednesday, 20 December 2016

I realize if I have to come back to normal, balanced thoughts, not overloaded emotional ones, I need to do a few things, including:

Find ways to still my mind: Entirely by chance, I came across a small Raza painting in a corner of an exhibition on Laxman Shrestha. It was subtle, contained and beautiful—gentle shades of grey and white, with the sentence: *Asatoma Sadgamaya, Tamasoma Jyotirgamaya, Mrityorma Amritamgamaya* at the bottom. It's an image I will hang in my mind to calm my thoughts and feelings and focus on inner stillness. Must go back and take a photo. Again, just divine providence that I came across it. I've also been chanting a lot, which is very soothing.

. . . **Reflection on 2016:** I think this is the year when I really made huge progress on distilling the drivers of my mental and emotional health. I have always maintained that mania and depressions are consequences of chemical imbalance, but the triggers are psychological, and I've always tried to understand my mind and its needs, more than its biochemistry.

This year, I stopped looking at mania and depression as discrete events, and more as a continuum. Earlier I would look at a particular manic episode and try and understand the causes. This retrospective analysis is of course important.

But what I see now is that there are at least four stages to this disorder: **Depression, Prevention of Mania, Managing Mania and Psychosis, and Maintaining well-being.** Being psychotic or manic or even depressed is not a flick of a switch, although sometimes it can feel like that. I realize I have to take active steps during each stage of that continuum to come back to equilibrium, especially when trying to maintain well-being or prevent hypomania, and be conscious of it at a daily level.

And I summarized the basic choice facing me as that between the 'vicious cycle of bipolarity' and the 'virtuous cycle of fulfilment', as a choice for a way of life. The goalposts shifted from avoiding mania and depression to finding fulfilment. What I was really looking for was a path to the virtuous cycle. Rather than looking at it as just a destination, I was interested in finding the road that led to it—the actions that would help me feel fulfilled, not just the outcome.

Seeking a path to fulfilment was an important milestone in my self-development. Happiness is not in the highs, I wrote in my journal. But I still wasn't clear on the actions that would lead me to feel fulfilled and happy. Six months later, I hurtled into hypomania, again.

Friday, 16 June 2017

I don't normally feel sorry for myself, but today is one of those days when I wish I wasn't bipolar. I don't want the passion, the emotion, the chemical khichdi, the roller-coaster moods, the soul, the heart, I really don't want any of it. I don't want to go to war with myself, I just want to be normal.

Two pieces of writing, a short speech at a family event and a poem, from June 2017 highlight how quickly creativity can turn from friend to foe.

London, June 2017

Hypomania alert—I am more energetic than usual, my mind is brimming with ideas, and I feel intensely 'connected' to the universe. I am in London with my family for a summer vacation. During this time, my family has organized a dinner to celebrate my aunt's fiftieth birthday. Normally, I would prepare a toast in advance. It would take me anywhere from half an hour to an hour, working on my computer, to complete it. But my mind is so preoccupied with itself that I cannot focus on the toast, and I walk into the restaurant empty-handed. Luckily, the restaurant is so beautifully decorated that I write a toast in a matter of minutes, frantically typing into my phone. This is the wonder of hypomania.

Desert Rose: A Tribute to Mamiji (Ruchi Kejriwal)

There's a piano playing jazz at the side of a private room in the heart of London, but the real melody is in the burst of romance that stretches along the length of the twenty-seater dining table.

Dozens of flowers, in a spectrum from scarlet to light pink sing in tune, celebrating the amazing grace of an amazing woman, my Mamiji.

The wooden table celebrates her inner strength, the scattered colourful balloons hanging from the ceiling circle the table in a warm and friendly way. Photographs are being clipped to tails of the balloons, highlighting precious milestones.

If there ever was a restaurant in any city or town across the world that captured a graceful lady's exquisite beauty, it is tonight, as we gather together to laugh, giggle and share memories of Mamiji's fifty years.

The only thing the table hasn't done so far is dance—and hopefully there might be some of that, either above the table or on the floor. Shah Rukh, Sufi or U2, it doesn't matter.

So this is an ode to Mamiji, who has nurtured, nourished and certainly overfed me all my life. Thank you for your love, kindness, compassion, humour and everything else you do to make life special for all of us. What an evening to remember, and it hasn't even really started. Could we raise a toast please for our daughter, didi, nanad, bhabhi and Mamiji?

I read out the toast but struggled to keep up with the conversations for the rest of the evening. I had already lost a lot of sleep over the previous fortnight. My mind was hazy and staying focused in the outside world was a challenge. And just a few days later, I wrote a very different piece, as below:

Prayaschit/Maut Kya Hai?

A soul chooses only its mother and its time of death
So as merchants of death
Maut kya hai?

Maut is ephemeral
Like the soul
Maut teen cheez hain

It is vakt—time of death
Itihaas ka ehsaas
Sach ka saamna
Shradha ki kshamata
Atma ki mukti
Shunya ki shakti aur shunya ki shanti

It is tareeka—mode of death

With honour
Like a samurai

With stealth
Like a jihadi

With cash
Lying back on tummy
Sucking a cunt

With shame
Dumped in a gutter

With corruption
Washed away in a river

With squatting
On expanding backyards

With grace
Waste to energy

And it is mauka—to redeem one's soul
So fuck tonight's deceased for all those you've fucked
Pluck the eyes for those you've blinded
And stab just as you would make love—all over

Humko man ki bhakti dena
Humko gun ki shakti dena

I know what I intended to say in this poem. It is about a
vigilante group that wants to serve God by attacking those it
considers to be immoral, according to its own code of ethics.
Death is about time, manner and opportunity, I conclude. But
I don't know where the piece came from. I have never been
violent during my manic episodes but they imbue me with a
level of aggression—and profanity. This is how hypomania
progresses into mania.

By August, even I needed a break, as I wrote:

14 August 2017

I'm feeling so much better. For the first time in a long time,
I want some respite from myself. The family does too,
but I really want some peace and calm for at least 6–12
months. Which means very simply, that I need to be calm
and peaceful every day, and every week, and then every
month. Be calm, peaceful, joyful and happy right now,
not go looking for it somewhere else, in the future.'

And I did find it—for some time. *Mint* published a year-end
piece by me called 'In search of my old self'. The descriptor
said it was about how 'rewinding in time to discover your
buried self can foster an incredible lightness of being',
through a regained sense of playfulness and spontaneity.[7]

But the cycle resurfaced in early 2018.

March 2018, Laax, Switzerland

I am in a winter wonderland and I am composing a voice note to Al Pacino on oil politics and terrorism. Next up is a dialogue with Shri Krishna Lord Bhagwanji. The children are learning to ski. It is meant to be a week-long family ski trip with me, Radhika, my cousin Nandini and our immediate families. But I am lost to the mountains and to my wayward thoughts.

'We've got our patterns now. When you're in that state, we let you do your thing, we let you do your walks and be by yourself as much as you want. And when you want to talk to us, we just sit there and listen to you. I think that's become how we handle it, just giving you your space, and Mom and Radhika keeping a close eye on you and talking straight with you when you need it and the rest of us just trying to keep that sense of normality for the kids and show them that it's not a problem,' says Amanda Meade, my sister Radhika's wife.

And then during the holiday, there is a moment that seems to change everything. We are relaxing in a café after the day's skiing. Well, the children are relaxing and drinking hot chocolates, I am struggling with images elating to my dharma. I experience a sudden and insistent urge to read my copy of the Bhagavad Gita (a translation by Graham M. Schweig, given to me by my Ajay Chacha). This is the first time I had brought it on a trip. Mania, after all, entails acting on impulses. We leave the café and head towards our apartment. I open the Gita and my fingers quickly rustle through the pages, on their own, before they land on three verses that are all about dharma. I have never read them before but they clarify so much.

'As the one without birth,
          the ever-present Self,
          as the supreme
          Lord of beings
Presiding over
          my own nature,
          I become fully
          manifest by Maya
          the very power of my Self.

Indeed, whenever there is
          a decline of dharma,
          O Bharata,
And an emerging
          of what opposes dharma—
          at that time I send forth my Self.

For protection of the virtuous,
          and for destruction of evil acts,
For the purpose of establishing dharma,
          I become fully manifest age after age.' [8]
          Bhagavad Gita (BG), Chapter 4, Verses 6–8

The footnote to the verses says: 'Maya is the supreme feminine power of Krishna by which he reveals himself to souls, as expressed in this verse, or conceals himself from souls who are not ready to know him (see BG 7.14–15). Maya is Krishna's divine illusive power, which either bewilders souls to facilitate their forgetfulness of divinity or facilitates the revelation of the intimate form of divinity.' [9]

I do not fully understand the meaning of the verses; for that I engage in a longer conversation with a learned swami many years later, where he explains that when evil tendencies rise, *spiritual birth can also take place within us through knowledge or spiritual practice. When we connect to the divinity within us, we find the strength to overcome these negativities and rise above them.*

At that moment in the ski resort, the references to dharma, Maya and the feminine power of Krishna provide me with a simple signpost: Krishna is telling me that my struggle to understand my dharma, which is the trigger of so much emotional turmoil and mania, is part of my journey to connect with the Lord himself. There is a purpose behind this madness. The message felt as direct as if He had texted me Himself.

I say a prayer, and then look up from the book, awed. Still hypomanic, I message a couple of my mentors about what just happened and then rejoin my family. The trip ends and we go back to Mumbai. On the flight home, I listen to bhajans throughout. Over the next few weeks, I reclaim my equilibrium on the balcony swing, where I spend long mornings, and eventually, get back to my daily routine.

Time seems to stand still during my recovery periods—my work and social calendar are quite empty. Exercising and spending a lot of time with the children help me find my mental bearings until I feel confident enough to interact with the outside world again.

Since March 2018 there have not been any manic episodes. There have been times when I have been anxious and lost sleep but not ascended into anything close to mania.

The seven therapies outlined in this book hold me together. The Bhagavad Gita moment, as I like to think of it, is one of those many blessings.

One of the most slothful days in recent times. I have literally struggled to get out of bed to play badminton and have slid right back into it after lunch, not having accomplished anything else. All I wanted to make sure was that I was up and about when the kids got home from school.

3 June 2019
(extract from journal)

3

Equilibrium . . . and Covid-19 (2018–present)

The invitation to join Soho House Mumbai felt like a miracle. Although located an hour's drive from my home, the private members' club was worth a weekly trek. I fell in love with its library, which soon became the genesis of many articles, and made some close friends. The turbulence of the ski trip earlier in the year had long receded. A pattern of mutually reinforcing activities had evolved. These included writing, teaching, speaking, some philanthropic giving, as well as family and social commitments and a fitness regime. A major wedding in the family in December also kept me busy, with dance rehearsals and wedding shopping dominating the calendar for the preceding several months.

Yet time is never linear, in my world. The amplitude and frequency of my highs and lows may have flattened, but they never disappear. For example, a few months later, I was overtaken by weeks of sluggishness, which led me to wonder if I was the same energetic person who once woke up at 6.30 a.m. to go horse-riding every weekend.

But I did get myself out of bed. 2019 was busy with new projects, especially in the area of education, some paid speaking engagements, philanthropy, travel and my book club and writers' group. This is what 'normality' tastes like, and it's sweet.

Some of the most memorable moments were exotic—in the summer of 2019, I persuaded Amit to come with me on a week-long cruise of the Arctic. Glaciers, walruses, breathtaking landscapes, champagne on ice and lots of chocolate cake—it made me want to visit Antarctica next!

But some of my most memorable moments were also the simplest. Amartya and I went shoe shopping in a mall towards the end of the year, followed by tea in a restaurant staffed by individuals with disabilities. I didn't often get one-on-one time with him at the time. And I wrote that day, 'he is just so mature, fun and enjoyable to be with', especially as he enjoys experimenting with food.

And then Covid struck, in March 2020. Nobody knew how long it would last, but I reiterated a basic message to myself in its early days: keep it together. If we are all cooped up and medical infrastructure is stretched and possibly inaccessible, I cannot afford to lose it. And I did keep it together, for the first wave. We were not torn apart by Covid in terms of human loss or job loss. Like the rest of the world, we adapted to physical confinement and online migration.

I suppose living with mood cycles positions one to adjust to the vicissitudes of a pandemic to some extent—I've learnt to expect change, not permanence. Even though emotions can devour me in the moment, I do somewhere know that neither the highs nor the lows are lasting. And similarly, with the pandemic, nothing is permanent. Lockdowns and periods of respite can appear and evaporate with little notice, and one simply has to adapt.

So when the opportunity to travel to the UK presented itself in late September 2020, I readily accompanied my mother to London to visit my sister, just before the UK's second lockdown. Being able to take daily walks in parks was a delight, as was catching up with friends. By November, life in Mumbai was much better. For a few months, I was back in the gym, at my beloved Soho House, at the salon, and I even celebrated my birthday with friends and with family at restaurants.

Of course, there have been times when I couldn't sleep in these last three years. One occasion had nothing to do with Covid and everything to do with a book deadline. In February 2021, I grew anxious about delivering the manuscript by the promised deadline and lost some sleep. My doctor recommended sleep medication, I consulted my agent and spoke with my editor, who extended the deadline, and a crisis was averted. My experience with quarantine a few months later was also initially stressful—some of our household staff tested positive. How should we quarantine them? Were my in-laws safe? How would we manage? Again, I took sleeping aids for a couple of nights until everything was settled. Knowing that I can access a good night's sleep if I need it delivers vital peace of mind.

But when the second wave hit in April 2021, I found myself in a new position of having to cope with intense emotion—sadness, anxiety, rage, frustration—on my own, with the children. My in-laws had tested positive and were in hospital, my sister-in-law and niece had also tested positive, Amit was self-isolating to protect me and the kids, as he had been in contact with his parents, so many people we knew were dying, I was losing sleep, pacing up and down the house, and writing poetry after a long time.

Boats

Death has not arrived at my doorstep
But it seems triumphant
Invading every inbox
With news of lives snatched before their time
Parents, grandparents, friends, colleagues
In their 40s to a healthy 90s

'We are all in the same storm,
But not all in the same boat'
Goes the saying
Some boats are drifting away
Never to return

Leaving only questions
Why her? Why him? Why now?
What more could we have done?
We are not prepared
We may never be prepared

Time stands still
Our hearts numb
Breath paused
Gut tight
Tears falling

And yet
Death cannot take with it our spirit
The power of prayer
The courage to continue
To light a lamp for those we loved
And celebrate their wondrous lives

Om Shanti Om.

I wrote 'Boats' to manage my own emotions, to reorder myself and find some solace. When I shared it on social media, I got hundreds of responses, which was overwhelming in itself. For example, an old friend said:

> It's a poignant reminder of the tragedy that is unfolding before our eyes. Very well-written. Stay safe.

One of Amit's colleagues, who lost three grandparents to the virus, messaged me:

> Dear Aparna, this is absolutely beautiful. And it is very helpful as we struggle with our emotions and fight to emerge from this stronger than before. Thank you so much for sharing this.

Another friend, who lost both parents to Covid-19, said:

> Aparna, thank you for your beautiful soul. You helped me to grieve.

A friend posted the poem as her WhatsApp display picture and another friend who runs the Asia Centre in South Asia included a verse from the poem in their newsletter. But some responses were more sceptical, prompting me to write another poem on the ground realities of the second wave, soon after I wrote 'Boats'.

Apocalypse, Now

'I love the smell of napalm in the morning',
The smell of victory
An epic line by a twisted Lt Colonel
From a frontline war movie
Apocalypse Now

But what about our frontline?
The smell of three-day-old bodies burnt in kerosene

The sight of living beings laid down, alive,
waiting in line for cremation
No money left for hospitals

The sound of mass sputtering
Cities gasping for breath

The touch of cremation volunteers
Dead bodies abandoned by their own children

Apocalypse, Now!
India burning
The taste of despair

Stay safe
But give big

A call to action
A channel for rage and helplessness
A small hope for ceasefire

I wanted to use it for crowdfunding but was told it was too
depressing and wouldn't motivate anyone to give funds.
So, a couple of weeks later, I wrote another poem, on the
importance of bereavement counselling, inspired by an
article I read in the *Mint Lounge*, a weekend supplement.

Talk to Me

When breath has collapsed
A hashtag is born
#covidorphan
Who will help them heal?

When death is abundant
A new term is coined
#vicarious grief
What will help us cope?

Talk To Me
A mental health NGO
A free counselling service
For the bereaved & grieving
For our Covid-impacted community

A call to action
A channel for rage and helplessness
A small act of solace

Stay safe
But give big
It's never too little
It's never too much

It worked. We raised more money than we had expected through a social media campaign and I was the biggest beneficiary, having channelled my emotional volatility into philanthropy.

I made it through the specific Covid week without letting my immediate family know that I was hanging by a thread. Prescribed medication helped me sleep. I went for long evening walks and did morning yoga. I wrote a lot and kept life simple so I could remain mindful and present with the children. This was a first: self-care, without relying on my caregivers.

* * *

The first lockdown gave me an opportunity to catch up on my reading, especially on mental health. One book, the slim but weighty *Strictly Bipolar* by psychoanalyst Darian Leader particularly left an impression. I highly recommend it.

Stress-related triggers and chemical reactions are key constituents of bipolar disorder, but I believe they are not entirely sufficient in explaining why manic depressives behave the way they do. Leader offers greater insight into this condition. He provides a deeper explanation of what he calls mania's 'signature motifs', those that distinguish it from other forms of mental illness. I can particularly relate to three of these motifs—'the sense of connectedness with other people and the world, the large appetite for words, and the attempted reinvention of oneself'[1]—I describe below how each of these manifests in my life.

For Leader, 'the manic person feels . . . wonderfully linked to the world rather than being its slave or its servant. The exhilaration that the sense of connectedness brings must be *communicated*, a detail that serves to distinguish true mania from states of elation in other cases . . . the key is whether the person has a sense that things are connected or not. Do they just love the sound of the bird singing, or, as well as loving it, do they feel it is linked to the car that went by or the article they read in the paper that morning?'[2]

To feel connected and to communicate—such familiar words! This is why I reach out to my mentors during these times, as I describe in a chapter on allies.

Leader also tackles the usual notion of 'flight of ideas' differently, by paying attention to the particular use of language amongst manic subjects. 'Mania was never a purely random flow of words, but had a real coherence and structure, yet one that was usually not obvious unless one listened very carefully,' he says. For him, 'mood is elevated because they are able to speak, rather than vice versa. It's not the mood that allows them to speak, but the speaking that liberates the mood'.[3]

'. . . the speaking that liberates the mood.' I have experienced this only too often. A few years ago, I was manic and attending a dinner party hosted by my mother at her home. As I flitted from friend to friend, cracking jokes, I heard one of them say, 'Aparna's on a roll tonight.' On another occasion, I attended a book club meeting in a similar mood. 'Aparna's on fire today,' said my friend, the host. Both times, language was malleable and I loved it. I've learnt to stay home now when I'm anywhere close to manic to avoid extra intellectual and sensory stimulation when I'm already burning up, but sometimes I miss living closer to the linguistic 'edge' of life.

Finally, Leader offers a compelling perspective on reinvention of oneself. Manic subjects are often described as thinking of themselves as the 'chosen one' or 'special' in some way. This may be construed as an egotistical reinvention of oneself. But Leader observes a different phenomenon. 'However egotistical the person's actions may seem, there is always someone there on the horizon. It has often been observed how the manic person tries to sweep other people up into some scheme or project, frequently with success. This is less about some private enterprise or solitary pursuit than a larger more encompassing endeavor, perhaps with a social good as its goal. Colleagues, friends and investors may be approached, and real things can and do happen.'[4]

This has also been my experience. Although I have often positioned myself in my imagination at the heart of a grand scheme to change the world (alas, without success!), aligning conglomerates and governments, the intent was to do good more than seek self-acclaim. To borrow Leader's terminology, my vision of the world was 'altruistic' and 'benign'.

● ● ●

So this is my story, two decades and many shades of light and darkness. It seems only fitting to end this section with a beginning, my first poem on my condition, when I knew I had problems with my moods and emotions but I wasn't officially diagnosed as bipolar.

Aquarius

A shoal of fish shimmers
A wave of gentle emotion

Sharks glide, menacing and toothy
Stabs of rage and frustration

Be still, my raging mind
The angry storm is not the only drumbeat
The constant tide has rhythm too

Gaze at the distant horizon
Touch those stranger shores
Stillness and movement in alternate breaths

Deep-sea divers watch their oxygen
Searching for sparkle in dark waters
Sifting treasure from insoluble residue

Moon and sun observe in rotations
Orchestrating highs and lows
Under a sheltering sky

But only the wind rubs boundaries with the ocean
An invisible companion,
Whispering shared songs,
In parallel journeys across the globe

I compare my mind with the ocean—full of waves, fish, sharks, treasure and rubble. The moon and sun refer to triggers for my internal conflict. The title is 'Aquarius' because that's my star sign and, of course, refers to water. 'Stillness and movement in alternate breaths' are references to yoga and staying calm amidst the turbulence. The 'wind' refers to my writing, my sadhana. That is all we have in the end.

A friend messages me to ask me what I'm working on. He is a creative director of an advertising agency back in Mumbai. I tell him I'm composing 'some poetry and imaginary dialogue for a screenplay I want to write'.

He writes back, 'It will be good. You have a roller-coaster brain.'

Probably the nicest description I can ask for.

Part II: The Seven Therapies

This is one of those days when I really miss London, and the collective wisdom and compassion of Dr Shanahan, my London friends, and Hampstead Heath to walk around.

28 September 2016

Sometimes it feels too much to handle—having to go to a psychiatrist, dermatologist, physiotherapist, endocrinologist, nutritionist. I guess this is what ageing and living with a mental health condition is all about.

10 March 2020
(extracts from journals)

4

Medical Therapies: Accepting the Difference between Personality and Illness

June 2013, London

Bright summer sunshine persuades me to walk, rather than take public transport, to visit a psychiatrist clinic in London, where I am seeking a second opinion on my mental health. It is now a few months since I have started medication under the care of Dr Sharma; thirteen years since my first manic episode. It might seem like an eternity to go untreated for so long but my situation is quite common. The median number of years between the onset of the first mental disorder and first treatment contact was eleven years in the US, says a study called 'Delays in Initial Treatment Contact After First Onset of a Mental Disorder'.[1] In India, the treatment gap for bipolar disorder is as high as 70.4 per cent, according to the NIMHANS report.[2]

So I walk into an unremarkable building in central London, breathing perhaps a little too heavily as I climb the multiple flights of stairs and enter a welcoming room with a desk and a sofa. Dr William Shanahan greets me with a friendly Irish accent. We discuss my medical, personal and professional history for an hour, after which he sends a letter to my physician and internal medicine specialist, Dr Jehangir Sorabjee, at Bombay Hospital, in Mumbai.

Date: 24 June 2013

Private & Confidential
Dr Jehangir Sorabjee
MD FRCP DTM&H
Hon Prof of Medicine
Bombay Hospital Institute of Medical Sciences

Dear Dr Sorabjee,

Re: Aparna Piramal Raje   Dob: 05.02.1976

Many thanks for referring this very pleasant woman who came along punctually on 24th June.

As you know she is a freelance journalist who is married with two small children aged 5 and 2. Sometime around the year 2000 she started having hypomanic episodes with intermittent bouts of depression. Some of the hypomanic episodes lasted up to six weeks but mostly around two. She saw a number of people and the general suggestion was that these were caused by life events and were more linked to her personality structure than anything else.

There was a tendency to avoid medication.

In February she had another episode that convinced her that this was indeed a medical condition and she agreed to go on medication. Her psychiatrist to whom she had been newly referred and whom she and her family like, started her on lithium along with a short course of a major tranquillizer for a while. She is now only taking the lithium.

She recognizes this as a big shift in that she now accepts that the diagnosis of Bipolar Affective Disorder is probably the right one for her.

Looking back she recognizes that the depressive episodes were always strange for her but she quite liked the times when she went slightly high. These tended to be accompanied by lack of sleep, excitation and a tendency to feel rather omnipotent and grandiose.

She had mild problems following the birth of her first child. Looking back she is able to attribute a lot of her problems to a lack of sleep and is clear that she benefits from eight hours rather than six or seven.

Since going on the lithium everything has improved. Her levels are good and blood testing indicates that there are no problems with her thyroid function or her renal functioning.

At present she is eating and sleeping well and she is enjoying her stay in London. Her husband Amit is extremely supportive and she believes that her marriage has given her a welcome structure. She has a very supportive family and is particularly close to her sister and her mother.

She doesn't smoke cigarettes and currently she is not drinking any alcohol. Street drugs are not a problem.

She enjoys life and is very sociable and keeps fit.

Her current system review shows no abnormalities.

On mental state examination, she presents as a bright and intelligent woman who makes good eye contact and a good rapport. Her mood is normal. She is not depressed or suicidal and she is not psychotic. Her cognitive state is normal.

She has a normal personality.

Diagnosis:

I believe the diagnosis is that of a Bipolar Affective Disorder. This is currently in remission. In my view she has been excellently managed by her current psychiatrist who has chosen medications wisely. Given the history that she describes I have no doubt that the prescription of lithium is the correct thing. She is well versed in her own early warning signs. There is a slim chance that she suffers any breakthrough hypomanic symptoms I would suggest that she returns to the use of a major tranquillizer for a few days until she feels well again.

You asked about alternatives to the lithium. I would suggest that she spends some time getting used to the lithium and watching her children grow up. She has a busy life. She herself is aware that she is inclined to put herself at moderate risk when she takes on big projects. Although she intends to balance her life as carefully as she can, she will undoubtedly find some of these projects quite exciting. I think while she is getting used to these, she should stay on the lithium.

I will be happy to see her from time to time when she is coming to London.

With many thanks and best wishes.

Yours sincerely,

Dr William Shanahan,
MB FRC Psych. DCH
Consultant Psychiatrist
Executive Medical Director
GMC No: 3221138

c.c. Aparna Piramal Raje

The diagnosis came as a relief in the end.

'She has a normal personality.' To my mind, this was the letter's most crucial statement. It served as a very important validation at the time, rather than believing I had a 'dysfunctional' personality, one that was only too often not in my control.

● ● ●

First Phase: 2002–2003

There were five phases of the search for mental health practitioners over the years. In the first couple of years, from the summer of 2000 to 2003, my family and I were simply scrambling to make sense of the situation. 'The doctors said that you were a borderline case and that you did not require any medication, even though your behaviour patterns had all the classic symptoms of bipolar disorder,' says my father, who was closely involved in my treatment at the time.

During this period, I met a Harvard psychiatrist on the HBS campus, where I was studying, whose name I can't recall now. He listened to my account and told me, 'I don't think you're bipolar. I think you just have trouble managing your emotions during times of major transitions.' This diagnosis felt reassuring—I felt 'normal', happy that I did not have a major mental health problem, but only some life issues that I needed to deal with. The doctor suggested counselling. I went to a few sessions with the campus counsellor, which were somewhat helpful. They enabled me to identify some of the triggers for my manic episode just before I joined business school. I also shared my coping mechanisms with depression (although neither my counsellor nor I referred to any of these shifts in mood as either mania or depression. I share some of these coping mechanisms in the chapter on self-therapy).

● ● ●

Second Phase: 2003–2013

But none of these efforts enabled me to come closer to understanding the root causes for my mood swings. I was aware of some triggers but I was no closer to grasping how to come to terms with them until my family was introduced to Radhika Sheth by my aunt, Swati Piramal, a qualified doctor herself. Radhika Sheth was her friend and an experienced psychotherapist. 'She has a particular skill which makes her a compassionate listener. I found that very good. I thought she'd be quite helpful,' says Swati Chachi. Back then, Radhika Sheth ran her practice from her home in Worli. I had graduated from business school and was working at the family's office furniture business when we first met.

Sceptical of the 'label' of bipolarity and of medication, Radhika Sheth's methodology was centred in psychotherapy, which was what our family sought at the time. Our sessions started with the four of us as a family, then in smaller combinations and progressed to me individually. 'From the first meeting, what I gathered was that you and your symptoms were a product of what was really happening in the larger circle, in the larger family dynamics. And that is why, if you remember, we did lots of family sessions,' she says.

'I felt that each one of you was revolving in their own orbit, each one was coming from a different world, each one wanted different things and needed to communicate that.

I also felt that when your family came in, they were hanging on to this very traditional Marwari family concept that everybody has to hang together, no matter what it is . . . those myths, which were not really working for you as individuals.'

She helped me tackle my most primeval emotions. I laughed, cried and vented out my anger, swearing silently in my head as I punched pillows in her home-office. Some of her most effective techniques involved role play and what she calls 'chair work'. She asked me to speak to an imaginary self or to someone else, as the case may be, sitting next to me on the sofa. I would then move to the other side of the sofa and respond from that person's point of view. I found I could dig deeper, to probe myself and my relationships.

'This is part of gestalt therapy and it helps you to deal with the issues of the past, or of the present, but in the here and now, in the present moment. So basically, whatever is happening at a subconscious level, is actually brought up to the conscious level. Once it's brought to the conscious level, you have a choice. Otherwise, you're continuously reacting exactly the same way that you've been doing all along, when something presses your buttons or when some memory pops up, whether you're aware or you're not aware of it. Once it comes to the conscious level and you're aware of it, then you have a choice either to do it the old way that you were doing or find a new way of handling the same situation or the same feelings or the same emotions. What was covert becomes more overt,' Radhika Sheth elaborates.

After visiting almost half a dozen mental health practitioners and with little to show for it, we had finally found someone who could help us. Warm and friendly, yet logical, firm and decisive in her reasoning, Radhika Sheth's approach was unambiguous—and life-changing. I came to rely on her to help me understand myself better and to examine why my mind was so often in a tailspin. Her support was explicit through the ups and the downs, and tacit through the welcome periods of extended stability.

As I stated earlier, this was a decade when I made life-altering decisions—the decision to marry someone from a very different world, my willingness to relocate to London temporarily, leaving the family business, give birth and raise a family, and eventually carve a new identity and profession for myself. Some of these became triggers for mood events. Therapy with Radhika Sheth made it easier to navigate these situations.

Her biggest contribution was a single line that remains a North Star for me: 'make friends with one's emotions'. Gain awareness of them and respond appropriately to challenging situations by acknowledging them, without judging or suppressing them.

'What works is to acknowledge that, "Yes, I feel this way. And now what do I want to do about it?" or "How can I manage it? Yes, I'm feeling angry. Yes, I'm feeling sad" . . . whatever it is,' she describes. For someone who was often overwhelmed by emotions—especially anger or frustration—this idea was a revelation and, in the long run, it led me to accept situations that I could not change with much greater equanimity.

Radhika Sheth did not dispute the need for medicines but questioned overreliance on them. 'Chemical imbalance is a reality and medicines are also important because you do need them and when you need them, you've got to take them. But to make them a lifelong crutch is a question mark. Because then you're not really using the opportunity to learn and grow, to understand your inner processes,' she says.

Instead, she introduced me to the Bihar School of Yoga through a young but mature teacher, Atmapadma (whom I will talk about more in later chapters). The goal was to help me evolve towards better awareness and better regulation of my emotions.

'I felt that underneath whatever was going on, there was also a very spiritually inclined person and somehow that need was not getting met. Yoga and breath awareness are a portal to higher awareness. According to yoga and the science of pranayam, disease is a manifestation of an imbalance of the pranas [breath/life force], of the flow of the pranas. Both body and mind are sustained by pranas. So there is a relationship between the body and the mind, and the influence of emotions on the breath. By working on the breath, you're changing its pattern and therefore it can change the state of the mind. And it is the same thing in yoga, when you're working on your body and you're changing your postures and you're changing your muscle tone, it's also changing the state of your mind.

'When a person comes in touch with the forces of the prana, he or she can learn slowly to control their mind, for it is tightly fastened to prana like a kite to a string. So in the same way, when you balance your pranas and you balance the energies in your body, it's like that kite, you're skilfully holding it straight and keeping your mind intact in the right direction,' Radhika Sheth explains.

I immersed myself in Bihar School of Yoga classes for a year in 2012 and found them very valuable, as I wrote in my journal in June 2012:

For me, the path of yoga, meditation and the ability to conquer 'the mind playing tricks on me' is critical: being able to observe my own emotions and thoughts, being able to take a step back, from both elation and demotivation.

And in November 2012:

> My yoga course has been enlightening: helping me to identify the root causes of my problems. I think my self-awareness has gone up considerably, and I'm able to better identify why I get stressed and what I can do to counter it. This is a huge self-realization: previously I have not delved deeply into the reasons for my stress.

Despite the progress that Radhika Sheth and I made, by February 2013 it was obvious that I could not avoid the 'label' of bipolarity any longer. As described in chapter two, I came back from the Bihar School of Yoga ashram completely unhinged—my mind scattered and all over the place—and was introduced to Dr Sharma. This was the third phase.

● ● ●

Third Phase: 2013–2021

Radhika Sheth gave me the psychological tools to have a deep and intricate awareness of my emotions. Now it was time to examine myself through a new prism of psychiatry and drug therapy. Dr Sharma instilled in me the confidence to accept bipolarity as a medical condition. As mentioned earlier, this acceptance came as a relief. I finally acknowledged that although my mind was leading me astray, it wasn't an inherent flaw in my personality, it was the powerful forces of chemical khichdi.

As I mentioned earlier, I was put on lithium, the most trusted drug for treating bipolarity, with some scepticism but minimal resistance on my part. Still coming to terms with the reality that my condition warranted daily, potentially lifelong medication, these two round white pills in any case soon became part of my nightly routine. A moment from early 2013 illustrates Amit and my joint approach to learning to live with bipolarity. One evening, I went to bed unable to remember whether I took my tablets or not (I did not have a pill box at the time). The next evening, both Amit and I produced one each of the same pill box—we had both gone independently to the chemist next door to invest in this essential accessory!

It took me a few months to become more comfortable with my condition. On one occasion, I had to fill in a medical form in the UK, which asked me to state if I had a 'severe mental illness'. Reluctantly and only after Dr Shanahan confirmed that bipolarity qualified for this categorization, did I fill it in. When asked if I took any prescribed medication, at the dentist or at the dermatologist for example, I hesitated before admitting to being on lithium.

'I think for a while you were anti-medication, you thought you would do all this on your own and the world would help. And then I think you began to realize that other people couldn't see it that way. And that maybe it was true that things had to be done to keep you well. I think once you accepted help and you accepted a range of advice, you looked at it almost like a smorgasbord of advice and picked the best suggestions that seemed to give you the answers you were looking for. So I think you're a much more rounded person after those years,' says Dr Shanahan, commenting on my evolution as a patient.

'You're getting the hang of the disorder,' said Dr Sharma at the time, adding, 'When you're taking on a project, just think: what's the price to pay for this? Will it keep me awake at night? If you're feeling creative and you're sleeping, it's fine. If you're feeling creative and you're not sleeping, that's not fine: take medicines.'

● ● ●

Fourth Phase: 2015–present

For the first eighteen months after taking lithium, I felt better, more content and at peace. But as I mentioned in chapter two, I relapsed in November 2014, followed by back-to-back episodes in 2015. In November 2015, Dr Sharma asked me to meet Suneeta Mehta, a psychiatric counsellor, as he felt I would benefit from talk therapy, not usually provided by psychiatrists. This was the fourth phase.

Suneeta's clinic, somewhat incongruously located in a jewellery district in south Mumbai, soon turned into a safe haven for me to share my thoughts and emotions. She also served as a conduit, liaising with Dr Sharma about my mental health so he could better adjust my medications. Over time, Suneeta became an anchor. The frequency of our meetings was fortnightly or monthly to begin with and much less frequently these days. We also communicate over WhatsApp. Regardless of frequency, I know I can rely on her. Her ability to sum up situations in simple sentences and her understanding of drug therapies are particularly useful traits, as I noted in my journal on 20 December 2016, when I was experiencing a burgeoning mood event.

> Suneeta's interventions are timely and transformational. I've been emailing and WhatsApping her on a few occasions, with the following responses:
>
> Keep up the hard work. It will take ten days to get back the balance. (empathetic)

I think you're still struggling with your thoughts. Please put some more effort into it. (matter of fact and encouraging).

Please focus on the real world. Put 100% into it. Then the unreal world will fade. (practical)
She's right on all counts. I find her extremely practical and matter of fact, and it really helps. She is the main reason I'm not on more medication and I'm so glad she's in my life.

. . . I realized if I have to come back to normal, balanced thoughts, not overloaded emotional ones, I need to do a few things: As Suneeta said, keep myself occupied with regular tasks, rather than the fantasy world. So I decided to go to the office instead of taking the week off as planned, sent the kids to Mom's, had a long meeting with a non-profit, focused on replying to many pending emails, filing remaining stories, had a piano lesson, went for walks.

. . . Suneeta's sessions were vital to my well-being. She's practical and knowledgeable about the disorder. And while she's generally very positive and supportive, she doesn't hesitate to be blunt when the situation calls for it. Just the fact that I can connect with her every fortnight for an update was a great way to channel my thoughts and to address any potential source of emotional stress or inner friction before it escalated.

Suneeta says she applied several techniques in our sessions. 'Cognitive behavioural therapy* gave you an insight into

---

* 'CBT [Cognitive behavioural therapy] is based on the theory that the way individuals perceive a situation is more closely connected to their reaction than the situation itself. Individuals' perceptions are often distorted and unhelpful, particularly when they are distressed. Cognitive Behavior Therapy helps people

your issues and helped you in getting more balanced with work and family. It enhanced your coping skills and involved changing the pattern of thinking, positively impacting interpersonal relationships.'

She also used interpersonal and social rhythm therapy (IPSRT),* commonly used to treat bipolar disorder, by working with biological and social rhythms. 'This therapy gave a bit more structure to your life. We worked on your sleep management skills and methods of controlling your triggers. You became better at managing conflict and we were able to avoid a manic episode.'

And finally, 'family-focused therapy: Working on communication methods, prioritizing family, and understanding your behavioural impact on the family were some of the activities we indulged in during this phase.

'These treatments not only improved your adherence to medication but increased your understanding of the illness. It helped in readjusting and recalibrating,

---

identify their distressing thoughts and evaluate how realistic the thoughts are. Then they learn to change their distorted thinking. When they think more realistically, they feel better. The emphasis is also consistently on solving problems and initiating behavioral changes,' says the Beck Institute, a non-profit committed to the training, practise and research of CBT.

* 'Social rhythms are patterns of habitual daily behaviors that may impact the timing of the circadian system directly or indirectly through light exposure. Social rhythm therapies (SRTs) support the implementation of regular, daily patterns of activity in order to facilitate recovery of circadian biological processes and also to improve mood. In a nutshell, SRTs encourage individuals with dysregulated mood to develop and maintain moderately active and consistent daily routines,' say the National Institutes of Health in the US.

eventually leading to the cognitive shift. We also had plenty of sessions with both you and Amit, and used support therapy as a tool to shape the conversations. Couples therapy acts as an emotional support system which gives long-lasting, positive results. One cannot overlook the contribution and help from your mother, who was understanding and cooperative.'

If psychotherapy and counselling provided me with emotional fortitude, then the drugs functioned as a safety net. On most nights, I sleep well. But on those rare nights in a given month when I may not, I know they are there to help me. Earlier, when my manic episodes were more frequent, they helped me to recover faster from them and promoted everyday equilibrium. These days, when I am more aware of my red flags, the medications prevent the build-up that could trigger hypomania or mania.

To begin with, it was just lithium. Dr Sharma also prescribed a major tranquillizer when I was manic. If there's ever an incentive to avoid getting manic, I believe it is that tranquillizer. It makes me woozy for several days at a time and inevitably results in weight gain. I was on lithium exclusively from February 2013 to November 2014, but the series of manic episodes from November 2014 to December 2015 convinced Dr Sharma that another drug was necessary to stabilize me.

I started taking an additional antipsychotic in early January 2016, with Dr Sharma slowly increasing the dose to therapeutic levels. Over the next several weeks, I just could not get a full night's rest (a situation that led me to empathize hugely with chronic insomniacs). Yet this was the one time when it seemed that the medication was losing the plot, not me, as seen in the incident below.

March 2016, Mumbai

'I'm not very well. I'm not sure I can do it,' I caution.

'Please do come. It will only be fifteen minutes. I'll receive you myself and we'll make sure you won't have to wait. We really want to hear from you,' the voice at the other end of the phone line attempts to reassure me. A senior communications manager at one of India's largest banks, Mr Saxena (name changed) has invited me to speak on Women's Day, to address a select group of their women employees.

But one look at my face as he sees me get out of the car and he suddenly seems much less confident. With good reason. I walk with heavy steps, the slow gait of someone who hasn't had a good night's sleep in weeks and has recently been injected with a lethal dose of restlessness—a combination that feels like the living dead.

I cannot sleep.

I cannot sit in one place for more than nine minutes (we time it).

I cannot work or read or watch TV.

I can just about eat a meal if it lasts less than nine minutes.

All I can do is pace around, lie down for a few minutes to take a break and then start pacing again.

Manic episodes usually creep up on you over a period of days but the restlessness I experience ambushes me all of a sudden, after a prolonged period of poor sleep. On the first day, we try everything to get me to relax. I get on the treadmill at a really low speed to tire myself out, go on a shopping expedition to buy table mats and even adopt an 'it's-never-too-late-to learn' attitude and attempt to play carrom—anything to divert me from the endless rounds of our living room, which I am circling with robotic efficiency.

So the decision of whether or not to speak in front of sixty women in the midst of grappling with some unknown mutation of my disorder, seemed, especially to my in-laws, obvious: Yes!

'You must do this,' my mother-in-law, Aai, and my father-in-law, Baba, tell me with a trademark combination of resilience, perseverance and stoicism that has propelled their family for the last four decades. Aai will accompany me, it was decided, just as she had come along to several of my functions in the past. I am a bit unsure but, encouraged by them, I decide to go—I do not have anything better to do in any case. And Aai, by now, was used to these talks; I have invited her on several occasions previously as I thought she would enjoy the outings.

We walk down the hallways of the bank into a large training room and we sit in the front row as I wait for my turn to speak. Of course, the wait is more than eight minutes and very soon I feel the restlessness encroach upon me. 'I can't sit here, Aai,' I tell her with urgent anxiety as she strokes my hand. 'Can we just walk in the hallways?' I ask Mr Saxena's team.

They nod and watch us going up and down the hallways until one of them approaches us. 'Since you're really not well, would you like to go to the sick room? We can send our doctor?'

'I won't be able to lie down but I can go to the sick room,' I reply. The sick room keys are located. I enter a compact room with a bunk bed, where I duly begin my circuits. Soon a young doctor enters. 'What the matter?' he asks in Hindi.

'I can't sit in one place,' I say.

'Then how do you work?' he asks.

'I don't work here. I'm a visitor,' I say.

'But what is the problem exactly?' he probes.

'Let it be,' I hedge until I finally admit, 'I have bipolar disorder.'

He looks at me and asks, 'What is that?'

In spite of the zombie haze, I chuckle to myself. 'Don't worry.'

And that's just one of the reasons I am writing this book.

I shouldn't have been surprised. The NIMHANS report finds that 'primary healthcare professionals are often inadequately trained, and reluctant or unable to detect, diagnose, or manage common mental disorders. Many people with mental health problems even experienced stigma within the healthcare services by healthcare providers.'[3]

Swati Chachi confirms that mental health is not necessarily a priority for all doctors. 'In medical school, mental health is taught by very few people. Not many people would even take up the subject. I also didn't really pay attention to it in medical school. We had many diseases to choose from and I was much more into chronic diseases, such as diabetes and cardiac disease. Watching you was an eye-opener for me. I realized that it was much more common than what we thought,' she says.

As for the talk? Did I do it? Of course! It was probably one of my shortest speeches but I'm pleased to say that references to resilience and my mother-in-law played a key role in it. A close friend, Upasana, who spoke at the same event but whom I didn't know at the time, later told me that it was pretty evident I was 'restless and keen to wrap up the event', but equally she could 'empathize and connect', having experienced restlessness and anxiety herself in the past.

In any case, the restlessness turned out to be akathisia, an allergic reaction to the antipsychotic and a frequent side effect of antipsychotic drugs. Mental health experts Jason Patel and Raman Marwaha, co-authors of *Akathisia*, write that 'akathisia is defined as an inability to remain still . . . The individual with akathisia will generally experience an intense sensation of unease or an inner restlessness that usually involves the lower extremities. This results in a compulsion to move. In most cases the movement is repetitive. The individual may cross, uncross, swing, or shift from one foot to the other. To the observer, this may appear as a persistent fidget.'[4]

From what I understand, doctors aren't sure exactly why these drugs have this side effect. Regardless, it was dire. There was a moment when I sat on my bed, with my head in my hands, saying to myself, 'I'm not sure how much more I can take of this'. Not knowing where the restlessness came from and how long it would last made it an even more fearsome adversary.

Since it was an allergic reaction, Dr Sharma was able to treat it with an antihistamine and by immediately discontinuing the medication. A milder variant reappeared a few days later but we treated it and soon I was back to normal.

The incident was bewildering. It made me realize just how powerful these antipsychotic drugs are and just how important it is to have medical therapies that are suited for you.

From the time that I started taking the drug, around 1 January 2016, till 10 March 2016, when I felt fully recovered, my medications were altered ten times by three medical practitioners—Dr Sharma, Dr Sorabjee and Dr Preeti Devnani, a sleep physician—all in search of a good night's rest. I was prescribed five different drugs, including antipsychotics, sedatives and antihistamines. Phew! I've learnt to ask about side effects every time I'm prescribed a new drug.

I continued with lithium, accompanied by an antihistamine to help with the sleep. In early January 2017, an antipsychotic was added to the cocktail. In July 2017, after another manic break, an additional antipsychotic and a mood stabilizer were added.

Finally, in January 2020, there was a silver lining. After two consecutive years of no manic breaks and four drugs every night, I was able to reverse the pattern of adding drugs to my nightly cocktail. We dropped one antipsychotic—I had been on a low dose for some time. It felt really good to be one drug down: as big an achievement as anything else in my life. In January 2021, we also reduced the dosage of the other antipsychotic and the mood stabilizer.

The side effects are sadly only too visible. I gained over fifteen kilos at my peak, my hair has thinned and lost its lustre and I am taking additional thyroid medication to counter the effects of the lithium. All of which is very disheartening. The weight gain in particular feels like a steady upwards trend that is hard to reverse—and I am not unique. 'Certain medical conditions which frequently co-occur in women with bipolar disorder are migraine, thyroid disease, and obesity,'[5] concludes a research study called 'Bipolar Disorder in Women'.

● ◉ ●

Fifth Phase: 2021–present

The fifth phase is the current phase. After nearly a decade with Dr Sharma, in early 2021 we decided it was time to switch to a new psychiatrist, Dr Zirak Marker. I remain grateful to Dr Sharma for my initiation into living with bipolarity but I was keen on seeing a doctor with a more holistic approach to mental health and well-being. My goal now is to calibrate the medication progressively, in conjunction with Dr Shanahan and Dr Marker, and come back to my post-pregnancy weight.

These experiences have led me to several conclusions.

The most important conclusion is that triggers are psychological; the brain's response is chemical. If I cannot sleep for five nights in a row, then the brain's response is chemical. But what's keeping me awake for five nights is

psychological. It sounds straightforward but it has taken me years of therapy to arrive at this conclusion.

Acceptance of the disorder allowed me to look at myself more objectively. I finally internalized that this is the way the cloth is cut. Awareness of my emotions, on its own, would not allow me to change the pattern of the cloth. Professional medical intervention was needed.

Reluctance to accept medication, inability to locate the right psychiatrist and discomfort with the term bipolar as a 'label' were the three main reasons it took over a decade to get on medication. I think my journey follows a standard trajectory for many patients with any disease or condition: an initial lack of understanding, a long search for a trusted practitioner, acceptance of diagnosis accompanied by relief and a subsequent attempt to manage the situation.

I'm not sure if there are any fundamental principles to short-circuit this journey but on the issue of the 'label', I think some of the best advice I received from a medical practitioner is the following: there is a fundamental difference between my personality and my illness. My illness may originate in the mind but it does not define me. It may occupy some part of my brain but it does not own it. Although being bipolar is an important aspect of who I am, it does not need to define who I am any more than the fact that I am married with two children and a hopeless cook are character-defining traits. It is simply a state of affairs I need to manage, just as one would deal with any challenge in one's personal life, such as physical health, relationships, money, career or other important aspects of individual well-being.

I'm now comfortable saying to myself:

o I take antipsychotics.
o I live with what's classified as a serious mental illness.

o   I visit a psychiatrist and a therapist.
o   And that's as normal for me as visiting any doctor.

'It's a contract of trust. What a patient is saying to the doctor is that "I'm relying upon your scientifically informed experience, from a good training, that you will make a diagnosis with me and prove your diagnosis through investigations if necessary and provide me with a treatment plan. And a care plan that will make a difference and make me feel better".

'But I think also recognizing the patient's own responsibilities in this one, they can't expect to be prescribed happiness, because no one has that in their gift. And that they have a responsibility to take the advice that they're given. And that they can be stubborn about it or if there are tablets involved, not put them in the bin and pretend you're taking them. If you don't want to take them, you have to say so. So there needs to be a fruitful dialogue. That's a two-way street,' says Dr Shanahan.

Equally, it's really important to talk. The 'talk' therapy helps prevent a situation where I'm awake for five nights in a row. It is vital to avoid escalating to chemical khichdi. I count myself lucky with my mental health practitioners. Radhika Sheth, who remains a friend, Dr Marker and Suneeta, who are my primary practitioners, and Dr Shanahan, whom I meet or speak with regularly. Four practitioners, when most patients struggle to see one (There is only one psychiatrist for over 2,00,000 people in India, according to a news report in the *Times of India*!).[6]

Which brings me to my conclusion. If you have a choice—and I'm very aware that many of us don't—try and find a mental health practitioner who will understand you without judging or offering stereotypical advice. A list of mental health services for patients and caregivers has been included at the end of the book.

For suggestions on therapists, look up Therapize. Matchmakers for therapy seekers and mental healthcare practitioners, as they like to call themselves, Therapize is a mental healthcare start-up that connects seekers and providers of therapy through their website, https://www.therapizeindia.com/. Therapize has connected more than 20,000 therapy seekers to a network of over 100 vetted therapists with diverse specialization areas.

Co-founder Anushka Kelkar was prompted to start the website in 2020, during the pandemic, along with her co-founder Aviva Bhansali, when they conducted an online survey of 600 young people and realized that most did not know whom to turn to for help for their mental health needs. 'What we found through our research was that a lot of people don't want a diagnosis; they're not ready for that. What they want though is to see a non-judgemental, safe expert who can work with them, walk them through what they're feeling and then eventually have a diagnosis, when it is required to get to that stage.

'There's often an intergenerational gap between care seekers and care practitioners. Mental health is very interlinked with cultural shifts as well and we found that there weren't many platforms catering to younger care seekers who are looking for open-minded practitioners who understand them. Over the last few years, several young therapists have invested in studying at top schools in India and across the globe and have been able to bring back a more holistic approach to treating mental health concerns. Unfortunately, finding these practitioners is not easy and when you combine that with the stigma of seeking therapy, often people choose not to get the help they require instead of going through the daunting process of finding the right therapist.'

Anushka also has specific advice on what makes the right therapist. The basics include confidentiality and ethics, being safe and trusted, and sharing a personal rapport. The second area is specialization—going to someone who can understand your issues. And finally, she emphasizes, the logistics—especially having an honest conversation on budgets.

'People are often very hesitant to ask questions because they feel that they may be perceived as stupid. But if their inhibitions and fears are not brought to the surface, the therapist can't work with them either. For example, something as simple as "Do you accept flexible payment structures?" For a lot of people, that's a really big concern. And they are not able to ask the therapist openly, "Would it be okay if I pay you in instalments? Do you do sliding-scale payments?" Therapists are usually very open to flexible payment structures,' she notes.

I wrote this poem when I first began taking medication. It marked my acceptance of bipolarity as a medical condition.

Chemical Khichdi: A Poem For Amit

Hormones and neurotransmitters,
This is entirely new terrain
Imbalances, synapses, major lapses,
The battleground is the brain.

The body is the poor victim
Responding to this deadly cocktail
—of misplaced intentions and actions
It can, alas, only fail!

Yoga asanas can, of course, help,
Head, heart and hand—all aligned
Relax, concentrate, focus on breath
But chemical khichdi is much less benign.

There is, thankfully, one solution,
To the doctors we must turn,
Hand over the reins, for a change,
There are many lessons I must learn.

Love, faith and courage
A solid foundation for a family
Trust, respect and adoration
You mean the whole world to me.

Vasant Panchami and Agastya was ready with his birthday present for me—a charming and detailed miniature study handmade out of foam board and a London bus in a half a globe. He is really something else. I loved the way he gave it to me too. He placed it on the bed when we were playing hide-and-seek, to surprise me when I was looking for him. These are the moments one never forgets.

30 January 2020

A long, lovely birthday lunch with friends at Soho House, with the very welcome sea breeze, special birthday messages, a surprise Middle Eastern goodie hamper from Chachi for an impromptu birthday dinner at home, streams of photos from Rads, morning hugs from Amit and the boys and the finale, a treasured digital card from Amartya late in the evening. This is happiness.

5 February 2021
(extracts from journals)

5

Love Therapy: Mental Health Is a Team Sport

January 2013, Mumbai

I am lying on a carpet on the floor in my sister's guest bedroom, trying to sleep. I have given up on the bed; it has given me no respite. Radhika and Amanda come in to check on me at intervals. The next morning, I go down to my mother's flat in the same family building, Piramal House, and spend my day cleaning and sorting piles of books. It keeps my body occupied without asking too much of my mind. When too many thoughts take over, I crouch in the guest bathroom and record them on my voice recorder, only to be deleted later. Mom, Radhika and Amit update each other on my progress through phone calls and taking turns to be with me.

Back home, my mother-in-law, Aai, father-in-law, Baba, and Amit are taking care of the kids and the home. We are very fortunate with our household staff—each one has been with us for years and has a vital role in keeping the household going, whatever the weather. My maternal, rustic nanny,

Champabai, and my versatile cook-and-housekeeper, Ramu, are particularly adept at managing the children in my absence and ensuring that their routine is not disturbed. Within a few days, I'll be back.

There is no doubt that we are an unusual family! My parents Dilip and Gita are divorced. My father is remarried to Shalini and they have a young daughter, Priyadarshini. My sister Radhika is openly gay and has a wife, Amanda. And I am bipolar, married to Amit who, as I mentioned earlier, is from a different background.

But this is not what makes us unusual, in my opinion. What makes us—and our extended family—unusual is how we have embraced mental illness as a family. We have accepted it, evolved practices to negotiate it and learnt to not just live with it but to *thrive with it*, just like in the case of any other disease. This is what I call 'love therapy'. To share how we got there, I would like to share perspectives from members of my immediate and extended family. It was not possible to interview everyone, especially the younger generation, but I have tried to include as many individuals as possible.

Amit is my best friend, philosopher and guide, as the expression goes. When we got married, our varied backgrounds led many to speculate that our marriage may not work. Living in a global city such as London for the first two years of our marriage, away from Mumbai's social requirements, we found common ground, built a foundation for our marriage and really got to know each other.

Bipolarity has tested that partnership. Before our wedding, I described my mood swings to Amit in detail but it was not diagnosed as a disorder then. For the first few years, Amit associated my manic episodes with life circumstances rather than mental illness. He then realized, along with everyone else, that it was more than that.

He faced sleepless nights. Physical exhaustion. The irrationality of temporary insanity. Mood swings. Listening to your spouse tell you that she wants to break up with you. Managing young children with a demanding career. And he has been solid throughout. I am deeply grateful for his unconditional love and support. His innate stability and security ground me.

For Amit, '. . . the episodes for me initially were confusing because I didn't know what suddenly changed you. There was sometimes anger because you had two little children and you were sometimes ignoring them. And I was worried because I felt you were interacting with the wrong people and you could have been taken for a ride. Also worried about what would be going through the kids' minds. There was also sadness for you—you were just not the same person that I interacted with during normal times. There was tiredness; it's not easy to keep this going for days together. I think there was a time once in 2018 when I didn't sleep for a couple of days at a stretch . . .

'First, I managed it by force. Taking away your phone, taking away your laptop, changing the passwords. But later when I realized that this was a disease, thanks to Dr Deshpande, I realized that all these are futile ways of dealing with the situation. At first, I was shocked but then I gravitated towards empathy and compassion,' he says.

He relied on family support, especially Mom and Radhika, to help me get better. But as my spouse and primary caregiver, the mood swings have also left him with one important realization: 'I am alone and others can only guide me. The impact of actions and the related consequences are entirely on me and our kids. So every step is like stepping on an eggshell. I have never felt so alone as during the episodes . . . But I have rationalized the situation in my mind. The fact that I have to go through fire during these testing times is very much a part of my life.'

Bipolarity has often assumed centre stage in our relationship, which has been difficult for both of us. 'It will be dishonest to say that there weren't times when I was frustrated and was thinking, "where have I landed up with this person?". I did mention to you in September 2018 that we can try to give the relationship a year and if you feel it is not working, we can separate. There was also a time when I felt that I should stay in the marriage only for the kids . . . otherwise there is nothing in it for me.'

But Aai persuaded him otherwise. 'Aai constantly told me that this girl has stood with you at all times. She has sacrificed a lot for you. You should not make casual calls and you have to wrestle through these situations, make it work for her and for the kids. I think she rightfully did the things that no other person could have done. Not to say that I would have been swayed to take the wrong decision . . . but it is extremely important that one of your biggest influencers keeps you on the right track,' he admits.

'Each relationship nurtures a strength or a weakness within you. I think our relationship, during good and rocky times, has nurtured only strengths. It has made me a mentally strong person. Every relationship is fraught with compromise. I think both of us have made compromises to stay together. I don't think I bring in all the virtues of a great husband that you would ideally like . . . Hopefully, we are two imperfect people . . . still enjoying being with each other. We have had some rough times but we did envelope ourselves with adequate affection immediately after the episodes,' he reflects. He ends with a most authentic insight, 'I strongly believe that a strong relationship is one when you still like the person when you are actually struggling to like the person.' In other words, a strong relationship is one where you continue to love your partner despite the differences you may have with them at a particular point in time.

For me, ongoing vigilance by my spouse can feel detrimental to the quality of our relationship. No one wants to be viewed as a patient. Thankfully, Amit has stopped asking me whether I take my meds but he still monitors the duration and quality of my sleep, even when I have learnt to take the necessary precautions on my own if I find myself going off track.

I would like to think—and hope—that the worst episodes are behind us. As Amit says, 'I never look backward. There is so much to look forward to. You can live life ONLY by looking forward.' Like other middle-aged, busy working couples, we do our best to make time for each other and as a family. Our most special moments are as a family. I'm a cricket atheist but the boys are cricket-crazy and play regularly with Amit, a former competitive bowler. I can't join them there but we do many other fun activities together—holidays and trips, watching movies, playing games at home or just mealtimes.

June 2017, London

Champabai, the boys and I are in a crowded London Underground carriage. We arrive at our station and I tell Champabai and nine-year-old Amartya, who are standing in front of me, to get off. They do. But my mind is so preoccupied and hypomanic that I am unable to get off the train in time myself. The carriage doors shut and the train lurches forward with six-year-old Agastya and me in it, leaving Amartya and Champabai on the platform. I gesture to him to stay put and

that I'm coming back. I get off at the next station and take the
train back to the previous one. Spiritual mantras are exploding
like fireworks in my head as I try and stay calm. Neither of
them has a mobile phone. Luckily, Amartya and Champabai
are standing exactly where I left them. It is one of the worst
moments in my bipolar life.

As much as Amit has tried to shield the children from my
fluctuations, the children have seen their mother behave
strangely at times. Agastya was very young during most
of my ups and downs and doesn't remember them. Both Aai
and Amit have told me how he asked for me when I was
away or tried to get me to pay attention to him, in vain,
when I was distracted.

Fourteen-year-old Amartya is perceptive and remembers
quite a lot. 'Mamma is in a funny mood,' he often said when
he was younger. 'Why are you so silent, Mamma?', 'Why are
you pacing up and down?', 'Why are your eyes red?' he has
noticed in the past.

Recently, I wanted the four of us to accompany some
friends on a ski trip to Kashmir. Amit was reluctant as
he didn't want to be in a 'conflict zone' if a mental health
situation arose. 'I don't know what's going on in her mind,
you don't know what's going on in her mind at those times,'
he explained to Amartya, who was present while we were
having the debate. And Amartya added, softly and gently,
'and she doesn't know what's going on in her mind either'.

So I asked Amartya how he felt when I was going
through 'a funny mood' and when I left home to go to
Piramal House or London. He says, 'At the time, I didn't
know much about the complexity of the situation, what you
were going through and how you were feeling. All I knew
was that they were called "funny moods" and you weren't

normal during that time. I felt concerned when you were going through your mood swings but other than that, to me, you were quite normal. You were also very open, which helped. When you left home to go to Piramal House and London, I felt a bit weird that "how can you just leave" and, as I was quite young, I wondered how you could keep going for a holiday to London suddenly to just meet your doctor. This was, of course, when I was young and didn't understand the situation. I also thought to myself when you were having a mood swing, "when will it end?".'

'I feel happy that Mamma has been better for the last four years and it's great that things are back to normal and that you have been good. I think you have been a great mother who has always been there and been very supportive and helpful. However, I think when you are normal and aren't going through your mood swings, you're much more rational and a much better mother than you already are. ☺☺☺☺☺☺☺ I also think that the past four years have gone by quickly and you feel much more fit mentally and physically in the last four years,' he observes.

'I know it's hard to manage a serious illness and much harder to manage a serious mental illness because it can't be cured by just taking medicines; it needs a lot more care. I think your doctors, Papa and you yourself are taking great care to prevent you from going back into that situation. It feels that you have just a little bit more weight on your shoulders because you have to manage your illness. But I think Papa and you have been really great about it and you've made sure that it is not impacting us in a major way. I also feel that while making a decision we need to just think a little bit more and take into account all the factors. This has helped by not rushing the decision and making the correct decision most of the time,' he says.

He and I shared a study while I wrote this book and I wanted to know how he felt about it. 'I think it's great that you are writing a book about your life and mental health. I feel your book can really help a lot of people and I bet a lot of people will be able to relate to what you were feeling. I am also glad that you are able to write a book about something you are quite passionate about and I really hope your book does well. Also, thanks for taking my interview,' he concludes. As a parent, I was impressed—and relieved—at his maturity and lack of judgement.

My in-laws Asha and Avinash are the last but far from least members of the Raje household. They have been living with us since 2014 and they exude a peaceful, undemanding and steadfast presence. Although Aai is not a very verbally or physically expressive person, I have held her hand when I've been crying and gone to sleep in her lap when I needed it.

I spoke with Aai about my bipolarity. Familiar with depression in a relative's son, she realizes that being bipolar is an illness and not a personality issue. 'I felt very sad when I saw you unwell but you used to get better too and Amit is strong; I knew he could handle it. Radhika explained to me that you have ups and downs,' she says, speaking in Hindi.

What lies unsaid is just how much she and Baba have influenced Amit. 'Aai taught me to be stoic in the face of adversity and Baba taught me to be open-minded. It is a very interesting combination. Not many people are lucky to have parents such as mine,' he says.

Next, the Piramal family. Radhika and I shared a blissful childhood. We grew up in a joint family and had plenty of cousins with whom to play. Summer vacations were spent in Europe, winters in Delhi, evenings at the racecourse or at the club. We loved our school and our friends—what more could we have asked for? Mom and Papa were role models, providers and just . . . fun-loving and caring parents, feminists, liberal, open-minded, creative, entrepreneurial global citizens.

Which is why accepting the divorce was tough. Life changed irrevocably. Ultimately it was the right outcome for all concerned and I am very happy now that my relationship with both my parents is harmonious. Yes, the separation was a trigger for some of my ups and downs but I think my bipolarity existed even before that and there have been many triggers since then. Mom, Papa and Radhika were involved with my care before my marriage in 2005. 'We tried to offer unconditional love and support by not being judgemental and providing the best medical advice,' says Papa. Since then, Mom, Radhika and Amit have been my primary caregivers.

Watching a child losing her mind is tough for any parent, as it was for Mom. She was quite reticent in sharing her thoughts and feelings about my bipolarity but says she often felt 'unqualified, uninitiated and helpless . . . I remember you once bouncing around in the living room and me getting increasingly worried. You were happy bouncing up and down but I was scared. That was my moment of realization that you needed proper medical attention'. Another time 'you were sobbing in a corner of your bedroom, near the door. You would not let me come near you and yet you were sobbing'.

I have often moved in with her for a few days to recover and spare the children my manic excesses. When asked what that is like for her, she says, 'Truthfully: anxiety. I never know what to expect. And I always feel I haven't got it right. On the other hand, just having you around is wonderful, both at your best and worst.'

A trio of caregivers is fortunate. 'What unites us is our love for you and the many, many joys and caring you bring to our family. Luckily, at least two of us, and often all three of us, were around to cast a safety net for you in the early-to-mid period. Taking turns is one of the early support we used to provide. Making sure you ate properly, that you took your meds even when you didn't want to. Sleep is always a difficult one; so simply sitting around until you fell asleep. You didn't make it easy but I believe we managed okay.'

Siblings (and their spouses) can play just as important a role as a parent. As I said earlier, Radhika and I are very close. We shared a room for years, studied at the same educational institutions, worked in the family business and are in touch almost every day, regardless of where we are. At her fortieth birthday party, I made a short speech, where I said, after joking about how she would regularly beat me up when we were kids, 'The sibling bond is really the most precious bond of all because it is the longest bond of our lives and truly special. All I can say is that with Radhika, I don't know where I end and she begins.'

For Radhika, what makes her well-placed to manage me during my mania is the trust we share. 'The unique relationship of a sibling is that a sibling does not have any expectations. As such, it is one of the easier relationships, unlike a spouse or a parent, it's easier just to give and take a bit. As a younger sibling, I've never had the feeling that I'm responsible for you. My goal is to help where I can. I think there is a very good trust level between us and there's no agenda, other than a bit of love and affection. There are no control issues. I never claimed to have authority over you. And that's why you trust me.'

A lighter touch also allows her to appreciate moments of levity. 'Your manic periods are not all intense. So even within the three days or seven days, there are up moments and down moments. It's not all bad. Like you're quite funny at times, maybe that's with hindsight?' Although she acknowledges the downs too. 'Mom and I have been in tears about you for hours.'

She can interpret warning signals. 'Reading your eyes is so easy for us now. We can tell whether it's going to be a one-week episode, three-week episode, from your eyes, your demeanour, your actions, the degree of mania, the degree of rambling, ranting. Are you throwing things versus just talking to your phone? Will listening to a one-hour bhajan calm you down? Will you talk into your phone or the voice notes for three hours versus five hours? Yeah, I mean, you really have a lot of energy. How copiously are you writing? Are you writing a hundred pages or ten pages? Amit and I are accustomed to having very practical conversations about whether he needs a break, depending on is it a relatively mild case or a strong one?'

She always wonders, though, 'How much control do you actually have in your mind? Because you have a very cheeky, naughty look in your eye. You know exactly what you're doing. It's not as much out of control . . . you can exercise restraint in the moment if you want to. That's a feeling I get.' And she's probably right. Manic highs are addictive.

Like Mom, she feels 'very touched that I'm able to help. I love being able to take care of you. I like being a reassuring presence in your life. Any time you come and spend time with me, I like it, even if it means that you're manic, it's never a problem'.

Reciprocity is key to making siblings so 'close, loving and invested in each other's well-being. It's about time, patience, love, lack of judgement, the way you would care for anyone who's sick,' she says. 'We've always been there for each other. Suppose you had been a very bullying older child who had always dismissed me or ignored me, then maybe I would not have reacted the same way. So why would I put in the effort every time and be there? Because I love you so much. And we've had so many good times together. The fear of losing that is real. If you're not well, if anything happens, that's a loss. That's my personal loss. But for distant siblings, they might not have that.' She is warm, empathetic but also refreshingly blunt—truly my Vitamin Rads. I miss her very much now that she and Amanda live in London.

Amanda moved to Mumbai in 2009 and quickly became a part of the family, taking care of the boys when I was unwell, which she says she enjoyed. She was new to mental illness too. 'I remember the first time you were sitting there in the chairs over by the windows and you were just talking and I didn't understand any of it. And you had this look on your face. Like, that was really the first time I've experienced somebody totally disassociated from their normal self. You were in a state of bliss, your cheeks were rosy and your eyes were far away, for the most part, and you were spinning tales and fantasies, which were just floating around . . . You're really in a different plane. Trying to communicate with you is very difficult. Mainly, I just tried to stay quiet and listen to you.'

Initially, not knowing me so well was a challenge. 'I do remember being nervous with you because I didn't know you as well. Now, I think I would be much better because I know you. I was a bit nervous when Radhika was at work and it was just you and I in the house because I thought, "How will I handle it, if something happens?" But overall, I just tried to be open and there for you.' Especially from Radhika's point of view, it is invaluable to have a spouse who is welcoming of her sister at these times.

April 2015, Mumbai

It is the proverbial 1 a.m. emergency call to Ajay Chacha from Amit. I am having one of my most manic episodes—I'm restless, pacing up and down the house, not willing to go to sleep. He comes over to our home, and both of them try and calm me down. He is back the next night. I wake up at some point in the night and see him sitting in an armchair, watching me as I sleep.

'I was a bit worried, as it was pretty late at night when Amit called but I also felt I needed to be strong and supportive because Amit was doing the heavy lifting. I felt sad seeing you the way you were but in retrospect it could've been much worse, you were not hysterical or anything like that, and I felt better that I came,' Chacha recalls.

'I remember the first time you came to me, back in 2000. We were sitting in the room next to the drawing room on the ground floor and it was early morning. I could not figure out what was happening to you. Because at that time, you were being very nice towards everybody. You were being the do-gooder for everybody. And you wanted to come for a walk or a ride with me. But then I figured out later what was going on . . . I have a habit of listening and I've always been fond of you. So I'm happy to talk to you and listen,' Chacha says. Providing a safe harbour for a volatile mind is one of the biggest gifts an extended family can offer. Chacha's calmness and ability to absorb even the most outrageous propositions, without judging, make him a great confidant.

As Swati Chachi notes, 'You utilized all the help that you could get, you also embraced the family values that you grew up with, you asked for help when you needed it, and Amit too. To ask for help takes a great deal of courage. Just maintaining those relationships with family has helped you.'

'You've grown up in my lap. And so when a child is in trouble, you almost feel like you get a stomach ache, it's so deep inside, the pain that child goes through. So I think that's what I felt when you had any kind of suffering. It would affect me.'

On one occasion, I burst into the home of my older aunt Urvi (whom we call Ma) in a manic mode, ranting and raving. She took it in her stride, without taking it to heart, realizing that I was not in control of my thoughts and actions.

My case has helped my family learn more about mental illness. 'I had actually never faced anything like that. So I never realized that if proper issues are identified, care given, it's something very manageable. Seeing it from so close, you realize that if you do it correctly, you can manage it quite well. And though that takes some time, for the realization to really come in, I found that if you give support, I think it helps. Basically, it's important to find the triggers and to get the right treatment in place, with family support and a stable environment,' says Ma.

Ruchi Mamiji reinforces this notion. 'You can just be there and not be judgemental. It has not changed the way I think of you or the way I feel about you. It's made me learn that if you are accepting of it and if you have good support from immediate family, you can still live the life you want.'

● ● ●

Love therapy offers some takeaways.

Here is a slightly tongue-in-cheek standard operating procedure (SOP) of five things to remember when manic or managing a manic person (strictly based on personal experience):

o   The smartphone is the ultimate weapon of self-destruction. Do not communicate with the outside world, even though every fibre of every brain cell is ordering you to do so. It will only lead to future embarrassment.

o   The voice recorder is the guardian angel of a manic person. Talk to it for as long as you need to; it will remember all those brilliant and compelling thoughts without judging you.

o   When a car breaks down, do you still ask it to run without fixing the problem? No, of course not. Similarly, when a person is hypomanic or manic, do not ask him/her any questions, specifically whether he/she has slept and for how long. One of the definitions of mania is that there are too many thoughts running around in one's head. Any external stimulation feels like an interruption that can't be easily handled.

o   Hugs are always welcome. Always. Even if the manic person in front of you is behaving irrationally, a hug is what he/she needs the most, as it will absorb emotion and relax the body. Massages are even better as they help release the body's extra energy.

o   Ride it out. This has happened and no amount of control or medication will make it stop in a matter of minutes or hours. In other words, we will have to wait until the tornado subsides. Unspoken kinship is the best. This way you are communicating that you care for the person, in the most helpful way possible.

Love therapy is a team sport. 'It is like looking after a patient. After the first few episodes we got the hang of it. We very much understood that there has to be a certain number of people, there has to be a schedule and there have to be shifts. We took turns because you are so intense that after four or five hours with you, you had to have four or five hours away, to just recover, relax, have a drink with friends and come back to the patient,' says Radhika.

During the lows, love therapy helped me overcome hopelessness in specific and practical ways, even when my family may not have known the true depths of my black hole. Back in 2013, Amit noticed that I was uncharacteristically quiet and withdrawn. We devised new career plans, for the umpteenth time, for what I could do to keep myself busy and mentally occupied. Mom instituted regular family lunches on Sundays, which I looked forward to during the week. Radhika freed up a cabin next to hers in the office so I had a space of my own to go to outside the house. We often ate lunch together and chatted about everyday life, as well as about how I was trying to get myself together.

With their laughter and spontaneity, Amartya and Agastya drew me back into the real world and helped me rediscover my centre of gravity. We made make-believe buses out of cardboard boxes and went camping in the living room with 'tents'. Their dinnertime was my favourite time of day; it introduced both structure and storytelling to my routine, both of which are essential when grappling with inner voids and vacant days.

Lastly, love therapists themselves need help. This is crucial. Mom, Radhika, Amanda and Amit confide in and vent to each other, of course, but they also have close friends, extended family and support systems of their own, which constitute 'safe spaces' for them to share their thoughts and feelings.

'Sometimes what a patient does or says can upset the caregiver. You have to reassure them that this is not what she is, this is not what she meant. It is just about having patience, having understanding, in listening and in not being critical. Maybe pointing out to the caregiver that there are other similar cases,' says Chacha.

Whilst support networks sustain my family, in general, caregivers of mental health patients have limited resources. Burnout is rampant. More than 90 per cent of patients with chronic mental illness live with their families, says an article titled 'Caring for the Family Caregivers of Persons with Mental Illness.'[1] It also underlines that almost 80 per cent of families experience caregiver burden.[2] As families become more nuclear, there are even fewer resources to care for the mentally unwell.

Caregiving also entails a significant financial burden. 'Most caregivers range between 25 and 54 years of age, with women accounting for more than half of those responsible for the duty. Usually, the caregivers have to forego [sic] jobs that could otherwise have brought in desperately needed wages, in addition to the mental strain that accompanies caregiving,' says an article titled 'The Unheard Voices of Women Caregivers for People with Mental Illness'.[3] Being able to fly around the world on short notice and take time off work to look after me is as unusual as our demographic composition.

Love therapy is, of course, not unique to us and we are far from perfect at it. Several beautiful mental health memoirs describe in detail how families support their loved ones. But my anecdotal experience suggests that love therapy is not as common as it should be, especially for Indian women dealing with mental illness.

A close friend was married to someone with a serious mental health condition. It was a toxic experience. 'There were symptoms even before my spouse's nervous breakdown but I was very young and didn't recognize them. After the breakdown, my spouse's family tried to blame me as well as my own family for his collapse. It was an extremely traumatic time, not just for my spouse but for me as well. It lasted many years. It's a very difficult position to be in—you don't want to leave the person who's suffering, you want to be their nurse or caretaker, but you don't understand how much you're suffering as well. When I eventually left, the trauma lasted for many years afterwards and I had to undergo psychoanalysis to understand what had happened,' she says.

She had to fight patriarchy. 'The conditions in India are very negative overall—mental health conditions are barely spoken about as there is huge stigma around them and families [especially prominent, wealthy ones] like to bury their heads in the sand like ostriches. Professionals in the fields of psychology, psychiatry and counselling are often not very professional at all—they turn out to be friends of the family and have vested interests. Where I did receive tremendous support was from my parents, especially my mother, who quickly understood the severity of the situation and the fact that staying on would have ruined my life. There was the added pressure to have children but I refused. Many women are unable to get a divorce as they have no home to return to—they feel abandoned all around but I was very lucky that this was not the case. The lack of support for women in India is astounding; patriarchy runs very deep.'

She recognizes that caregivers 'need to be understood too. There needs to be transparency, trust and care in every direction. I find the culture in India extremely judgemental on so many levels. There needs to be an infrastructure within the family, which provides a sense of shelter rather than criticism'.

Instead, the family was in 'complete denial and he was quickly married off soon after our divorce. It's all about maintaining an appearance of credibility, rather than excavating the real causes behind emotional and mental suffering . . . We need to educate ourselves, accept that mental health conditions are present in different forms in friends, family members or acquaintances all around us, gain the necessary tools to identify them, not judge, and then see how to cope. All healing starts at home, within a space where one is meant to feel safe and protected'.

Another friend grew up with a bipolar father. There was a history of depression on the father's side of the family but her father's condition was never explained to the children. She describes how her father would sometimes disappear for weeks at a time to travel and meet his friends when he was in an excited mood, without letting the family know where he'd gone, only to return in a depressed mood, listening to sad songs on a continuous loop and crying in a corner of the drawing room, while the children were expected to get on with their homework in the same room.

'I remember in class eight I had been asked to write an essay on the person I admire the most, in the school exam. And I wrote about my father. The first few lines of that essay were that "he has not climbed any high mountain or forded any deep rivers but he battles depression every day. And for me, that is the mark that he has courage. And he's a person to admire".' She showed the essay to her mother but not her father.

The illness was brushed over rather than approached with empathy or loving support, she recollects. As an adult, she realizes how much the ecosystem matters for anyone coping with a mental health condition and how important it is for parents to explain these matters to children.

I would like to end on a more optimistic note, with three suggestions for caregivers, which I call the three Ts: trust, trigger management and therapy. Caregivers can only be effective if their patients trust them. Building this trust during times of equilibrium can enable a caregiver to be better heard during times of stress. Try deepening your relationship when the patient is well, as much as you can. Family acceptance of mental health conditions is also an essential foundation of trust, so that the patient feels understood.

Caregivers are uniquely placed to spot triggers and to arrest a situation before it escalates. By now, I am well versed in my warning signals but for many years that role fell to my immediate family members and, sometimes, to my close friends.

And therapy or rather conventional therapy and counselling. Amit has often visited my counsellor Suneeta on his own. She is as available to him as she is to me. Caregiving asks a lot from loved ones. They need their sources of nourishment too.

Finally, a poem I wrote for Amit, and one for the boys, which tries to explain bipolarity to young children.

Lithium

This disorder is a sea-creature
Hovering just beneath the surface
I can go under without warning

You are not just my rock
You are more than my lighthouse
We float our boat together

For every flame
Which scorches me with its heat
And then expels me into its shadows

There is also illumination
When there is you.
When there is us.

There's a Tigress in My Bedroom

Shhh! Let me share a secret
Not many people know
There's a tigress in my bedroom
An invisible tigress
I'm her only special friend

The funny thing about this tigress
Is that her moods change
So I don't always know what to expect
When I go into the bedroom

Sometimes she's mad
Sometime she's sad
Sometimes she's very funny
Even playful as a kitten
Mostly she's just quite cuddly

Her roar energizes me
She's taken me for wild rides
We go higher and higher
Spiralling out of control
Like the rodeo at the school fete

It's fun at the beginning
But the falls are rough
Getting up is always tough
I even wondered once if she was dead
But she finally raised her furry head
I'm still here, she said.

I want to tell others about her
But since she's invisible you see
To everyone apart from me
I thought if I took a photo of her
Someone might believe me

So I took one—but she vanished from the image
I dragged her in front of the mirror
And couldn't find her there either
And that's when I realized
The tigress isn't in the bedroom

She's in my tummy, when it explodes
She's in my head, when it spins
She's in my heart, when it bursts
—with tears of joy or pain or both

And that's when I realized
If I am sad, her tail will flop too
If I want to get high, she'll give me a ride
But we will eventually crash

So now I'm just friends with her,
I lie against her, rub her neck
Laugh, smile, tickle, giggle or cry
Bury my head in her fur when I'm angry or scared
Make friends with my most intense feelings

For that's what the tigress is.
She is my tigress,
She is my emotions
But she is not me.

Now you know my secret
There's a tigress in the bedroom
And there's much more to me

I need someone competent to advise me. [My writing mentor] Khozem is the right place to start and for that I'm so grateful.

1 August 2018

I love my friends. I have to say this again: **I love my friends.** From Pooja S., who met me at night, to Seema and her voice messages, to my bipolar girl power group, to Radhika Desai who I sobbed over the phone with, to Tanya and Hetal's comforting wisdom, to just so many of them. I am so, so blessed to have them in my life.

20 November 2017

Allies help me to negotiate my emotions; they help me fight a war. If it takes a lot to be a friend, it takes a helluva lot of friendship to be an ally.

12 November 2018
(extracts from journals)

6

Allies and the Therapy of Empathy

January 2006, Mumbai

It is late evening. I have been struggling with mania for a few days. The wind seems as possessed as my racing mind; the clouds seem to swirl with just as much darkness as my demons. I share one of my mental nightmares with one of my mentors, through a series of frantic text messages.

I receive a single reply, 'The person who copes with this trauma is very brave.' I see it and reply, 'XYZ, thank you.' That's what I need, to get me through this particular night.

This, for me, is the power of mentors.

The word 'ally' is commonly used to describe friendly nations who come together in wartime to protect one another. It is particularly appropriate for someone with a mental health condition such as mine, which often feels like a psychological and physiological civil war. My allies—consisting of my mentors, friends and networks—shelter me during wartime and nourish me during peacetime.

No one more than Khozem. In his fifties, Khozem is a former journalist from the UK and an erstwhile colleague of my mother's, from her time as a journalist with the London-based *Financial Times*. Now based in Mumbai, he embodies the two cultures that I grew up in, Indian and English. He has also worked extensively in both journalism and business and is one of my most trusted mentors. I gravitated towards our overlapping sense of kinship and for a period of five or six years, he found himself at the receiving end of a lot of my manic writing. The subjects ranged from politics and world affairs to religion and spirituality to film-making—and my sexual trauma-related psychosis.

'I've got the voice notes, the pen drives, the manuscripts. The recordings occasionally felt like 2 or 3 a.m. meanderings but the writing was particularly good because it combined discipline with insight, it combined clarity of expression with perception and it was genuinely deep. It was good quality self-examination that wasn't vain but was descriptive and intelligent. There are so many charlatans out there,' he says, explaining why he was always willing to receive it.

'But it quickly evolved from there to the other pole—articulation of someone in some deep distress, like they were coming from the deep bowels of your body. The writing now strikes me as being quite pained,' he observes.

As I wrote earlier on, mania (and particularly psychosis) can be extremely traumatic. It is like being trapped in a cinema that is showing your worst horror movie, 24/7. Unlike watching a movie, you cannot shut your eyes and ears. There is no escape. Your thoughts will haunt you in the darkness and continue to blind you in the light. The voices in your head cannot be switched off so easily. My favourite bipolar joke makes light of this: the trouble with being bipolar, you can't take your mind off it! You just have to deal with the nightmare until it subsides.

And what a nightmare it can be. As I mentioned earlier, I experienced relentless scenes of rape, murder, incest and sexual torture for several days at a time on the half a dozen occasions when I was manic or psychotic during my mid-twenties to late thirties. I imagined scenes of sexual violence involving people I know—both as victim and as perpetrator—and in some instances, I felt as if I were living through those experiences. The reasons these psychosis-induced memories are relevant here is that they illustrate a vital aspect about coping with bipolarity: the role of the wider community as allies. *If it takes a village to raise a child, it takes a community of allies to heal a mind.*

It is because I have learnt to witness my most private vulnerabilities, to detach from the most sickening recesses of my mind and to document the most poisonous residues of my brain, that I enjoy periods of stability. What has enabled me to get to this place, when I can *witness, detach* and *document*? There are several factors, including my spiritual therapy, but I would like to highlight the role of my mentors and what I call the 'therapy of empathy'.

Like Khozem, I confided in a few mentors during my most vulnerable moments. They share several common characteristics. They are all fifteen to twenty years older than me. They are men and women—this is not a gender issue. Some are family friends with whom I had established an individual rapport, others professional mentors or both. None have any professional qualifications or background in mental healthcare. They respond to me based on their own instincts and experiences. They are empathetic, intelligent, mature, compassionate, sensitive and, of course, trustworthy. Since they were already mentors, in my inner circle, it felt natural—and safe—reaching out to them.

They helped in a number of ways, but especially during a manic phase.

During these times, or right after, I would often reach out to these individuals—some in person, others over the phone or through voice or written notes, documenting what I was going through, sharing exactly what was plaguing me. Their responses were fairly standardized—after a deep intake of breath, they would say something to the effect of: 'Are you okay? I am traumatized listening to what you have just told me.'

And I would reply: 'I'm better now, thank you.' For me, the danger was real, even though it was just in my mind, and it meant so much that someone could understand my pain, without questioning its provenance.

Just to be able to tell someone: 'I'm going through hell. I want you to know it. The fact that I have the self-awareness to tell you what I'm going through is, for me, one step towards coming to terms with it. It may torment me right now but I am determined not to let this hell take over my sanity permanently.'

They absorbed all of it, without reacting, without judgement. Had they said: 'Aparna, are you crazy? Are you insane? Are you sick? Let's get a doctor. Let's call your family. You need help,' I would have stopped opening up to them. There was none of that, even though I was clearly mentally unstable at the time and needed medical help (There have been some occasions when a mentor reached out to my family members, expressing concern for my mental health, but in general their role was to hear me out rather than intervene).

The art of empathy is much debated in today's world, by advocates and sceptics. For some commentators, it defines our current existence; for others, it is highly overrated. For me, empathy rests primarily in being able to listen and absorb, without necessarily reacting. I believe we live in a world where opinions are a commodity, where reactions are reflexive but listening is rare. My mentors listened, they waited and they watched as the situation unfolded, even when they may not have understood it.

Such as Tarun, one of my oldest mentors. A strategic brand and marketing consultant, Tarun and his wife Shanthi adopted me as a family member over twenty years ago, when I was Tarun's client. Tarun says, 'Initially, I would wonder, what's wrong with her? After speaking with Amit, I realized it's an issue. Then I started holding on to you more. We spoke a lot. You told me bizarre things. I would listen. I would never cut you off. And I don't remember in that conversation if I ever asked you a question. Those conversations were very intense and you had a habit of taking down notes. There were days when you called up and you were very angry, some days happy, but most times angry. I never understood why my number was on your phone, why I was part of the mix, but I never questioned it either.'

Their empathy was not restricted to managing mania. Some of them actively reached out to me during my depressive phases too. For example, one kept inviting me to join WhatsApp when it first launched, until I did, so that he could send me motivational messages on a fortnightly basis, to cheer me through my depression. Another mentor ran into me at a party and asked me a blunt question: 'Nobody doubts that Aparna can manage her emotions. The question is—does she want to?' It compelled me to examine how much I liked being 'high'.

Khozem treated me to endless rounds of green tea every few months, for what must have seemed like a decade, helping me to transition into journalism, find my writing voice, to shed skin where needed and look inwards. Meeting him became a post-recovery ritual after a manic episode.

When it was first apparent that I would have to switch from business to journalism as a full-time profession, he and I met at the Willingdon Club and he took me through what it takes to be an independent freelancer. 'You're looking too fearful at the prospect,' he commented at the time. A few years later, when I had sent over too many manuscripts and voice notes, he sat me down at the Bombay Canteen restaurant and pointed out simply and practically how I could learn to live a fuller and richer life in the 'real' world so that I wouldn't need to spend so much time 'in my head'. 'Have dinner parties with your creative and design world friends, travel to lit fests with your book club, host salons, go to music concerts,' he urged. I was so numb and dejected; I could not grasp what it meant to channel my intellectual energies in a fruitful way. But the conversation seeped into my consciousness.

What did these mentors provide that my family, friends and mental health practitioners could not? Mania and psychosis, as I have mentioned earlier, are extremely frightening to all concerned. In this situation, the main role of primary caregivers and mental health practitioners is to help me stabilize—they need to 'fix' the situation, through medication, rest and a quiet, stress-free environment. Had I shared my mental trauma with any of these parties, it would have led them to panic even further. If my outward symptoms are so stressful, you can only imagine how they would react to my nightmarish inner world.

What I needed was someone who was willing to listen but was not expected to necessarily react. Family members and mental health practitioners do not have that luxury. As primary caregivers, they are, quite rightfully, compelled to react and get the mania under control.

Mentors, on the other hand, are placed at that little bit of distance from the heart of the storm, which affords them some perspective. As much as my doctors sought to protect me from the most jagged edges of my mind, my mentors empowered me with the insight: 'If you want to spit this venom out of your head, you know I can swallow whatever you send my way.' For me, this dichotomy is mutually reinforcing and helps to heal.

It is one of the many reasons that the horror of psychosis doesn't make me cry. It is a multiheaded sea monster that lies somewhere deep within me. I must be vigilant not to awaken it; I am wary of its power, but not fearful, bitter or sorrowful about its existence.

Mentors have also been true allies to my immediate family. For example, a few years ago, Amit arranged for me to stay the night with mentors Sanjayji, a senior journalist, and Shanuji, his wife, when I was manic. He wanted to shield the children from me and also thought I might listen more to Sanjayji and Shanuji, a couple whom Amit and I meet regularly and who are also family friends of my mother. It was a new situation for them. Sanjayji told me they were not quite sure how they would ensure I got a good night's rest and that I wasn't talking to myself. He remained watchful through the night. Even though I crept into the bathroom to continue talking to myself at one point in the night, I knew that they were looking out for me, and I was definitely more composed the next day—just like I'm sure everyone at home was a lot more rested.

On another occasion, mentor, investment banker, workaholic and close family friend Rajeev left his office in the middle of the day to persuade me to leave a Starbucks café, where I was fixated, not listening to Amit, intent on going to a meeting that didn't exist.

Elsewhere, Dr Raman, a cancer surgeon and one of Amit's most cherished mentors, helped to connect us to my first psychiatrist. He is also one of the few individuals who sees the humour in my manic moments. 'Combining an ability to see humour in most situations, along with a medical problem-solving ability, is required in assisting recovery from both physical and psychological problems. Everyone who approaches for help has a reality of their own and to bring them back from it and accept progress in small steps—however small—needs patience, empathy and compassion, not pity,' he says.

As another mentor and former journalist Manjeet observes, Amit 'used whatever helping hands were around him to be able to join a circle of trust and understanding that could embrace you through this struggle'. Manjeet Mausi, as I refer to her, is also one of my mother's friends and a trusted confidante. My mother has been very generous with her friends!

● ● ●

Close friends are my second type of allies. To quote Virginia Woolf, 'Some people go to priests; some to poetry; I to my friends.'

I've tried to maintain friendships from throughout my life—from high school in Mumbai, and school and college in the UK to business school in the US, the mothers of my sons' classmates, the next-door neighbours as well as professional acquaintances who became close and more. Today, these friends might be sprinkled across the globe, from Mumbai to London, to Dubai, San Francisco and rural Vermont, but we stay in touch. They have seen me in all my avatars—mostly stable, but every so often, manic or depressed. Mentors and friends share many common characteristics, but as friends are the same age as me, they are often more involved in my daily life than mentors. To the best of my knowledge, I have spared them the extremities of my horrors.

I spoke with a few friends in particular who have helped me weather my ups and downs over time, to understand what it takes to be a good friend to someone with a mental health condition.

There are so many ways to help! Collectively, this is the therapy of empathy.

Some friends provide a safe haven, quite literally. One of my oldest school friends, Saumya, reminded me of a time in the early 2000s when I showed up with a suitcase at her home, ready to move in for a few days because I was going through some turbulence and felt I needed space from the home environment. She was living in the US at the time and wasn't even home when I came over but her apartment was a safe haven. Her father indulged my insistent requests, which included escorting me to Chowpatty for Ganpati darshan and holding my hand really tight to make sure I didn't melt into the crowd. Although it was twenty years ago, I remember how magical the festival seemed that evening, pulsating with a special energy concocted by my hypomanic imagination.

On another occasion, when there were too many thoughts running through my head, I climbed the jungle gym in the children's playground in Saumya's building to find a place to escape from them. She followed me, sitting at the top of the jungle gym, waiting in silence until I was ready to climb back down. She has often come over when I'm going through a manic episode. The funny thing is, I can't remember what she said on any of those occasions but I know how comforted I was by her presence.

It's not always possible to move in with a friend but friends can always listen. Just like mentors, some of them have turned listening into an art form. My former neighbour, Pooja, believes, 'I think the main thing is to listen and be calm because you can't do anything else at that point of time. There's nothing you can do when a person is so upset, no matter what you tell them, they're not going to understand. The next day, you can have a conversation about it and discuss it, which we used to do all the time.'

In a time-strapped world, just being available is invaluable. Pooja recalls a day when I said, 'I'm just coming to your house right now.' She was nursing newborn twins, and I showed up in her bedroom and cried for half an hour. She didn't know how to react, she says, especially as she was with the babies but she waited until I regained my composure. For me, being able to go over to someone's home at the exact moment when the dam burst was priceless.

Friends can expand their understanding of how to manage the disorder. Saumya told me, 'Over time, as I researched and read more about supporting loved ones with bipolar disorder, I made a conscious effort to prioritize encouragement over advice, saying "I'm here for you", "I care", or "even though I don't fully understand, I can offer my support". I've learnt to be patient with and understanding of your mood episodes and tried to make you really feel heard by truly listening to you actively instead of passively—making eye contact, affirming what you said with feedback like nodding and asking clarifying questions. I stay away from platitudes like "calm down" or "cheer up".'

Very importantly, friends withhold judgement. An old friend Rahila says it's vital 'not to be judgemental and opinionated. If you tell me something when you're going through a peak, I'm not going to hold that against you. I know you're going through a phase and you need leeway'.

Some of my friends have learnt to strike a balance between maintaining my confidence and communicating with Amit.

My high-school friend Shama says that she reached out to Amit on a few occasions when she felt I was headed for an incident. 'I think the first time I seemed to be more aware and so I think it raised a red flag for him.' Equally, she says, 'Sometimes I haven't. And I wonder sometimes if I should have done it.'

Like mentors, friends help the family. Once I remember being taken to the doctor. The music was on in the car and I was singing loudly, oblivious to Amit, who was trying to cope with my volatility. To my right was another one of my oldest friends, Shazia, trying to assert a calming presence. 'I normally get called in when everyone's having a real bad day, which I don't mind. It just involves me kind of sitting with you or hanging about with you or listening to music with you or going to the doctor. And so I feel that my role at that time is just to help out whenever they ask. As part of being a very close friend. So if any time they need help, or you need help, I'll always help,' she says.

Close friends have even learnt to have fun during these crazy times—mania is, after all, a high for much of the time. As Rahila says, 'You've been absolutely unreasonable at times and I've gone along with the fun of it. I've had fun with you in the conversation but then I steer you also, to look at it differently. So the reason you will open up and talk to me about stuff is because one, I'm not judging. And two, I'm having fun along with it. And yet, I am guarding that secret of yours as well as making sure that I'm having a parallel conversation with someone saying that "hey, something needs to be done. She's not absolutely stable".'

For Saumya, fun is encouraging me to do activities that I find enjoyable or relaxing—walking together, listening to nostalgic music, napping, shoulder rubs or head massages. This one-on-one girlfriend time is particularly helpful during depression.

One of the most important ways a friend can help might seem to be the most pedestrian but is actually a lifeline—by being 'the daily download friend' with whom I can download my everyday thoughts and feelings, such as fellow class mother Ankita. 'It's become a habit to send messages asking how your day was, sharing a one-minute summary of my day. It feels good letting go of one's thoughts. I look forward to reading what you write, the small things,' she says. As do I. We live in a world where it's often easier to have a conversation about the big things in life over a scheduled lunch or dinner than the daily trivia of everyday life.

Even though she lives on the other side of the world, in a totally different time zone in San Francisco, my school friend Seema Bhangar and I swap voice notes on our daily joys and frustrations. Waking up to her messages is a much-anticipated morning ritual. Having someone to share these feelings with is nothing short of a miracle in keeping my emotional barometer stable. It prevents escalation of moods and is incredibly therapeutic. Only a few friends have the time, patience, inclination, sensitivity and ability to respond to my daily vicissitudes and Seema is one such gem.

Telling your friends that you're bipolar can be an important milestone in the relationship. My Harvard roommate, Louise, was slightly tearful when I told her over breakfast in a café in London, many years after we left business school. 'I thought I knew you but we hadn't seen each other physically for a long time. I was moved for you, that you would have to be cognizant of it for the rest of your life in a way that you hadn't had to before,' she says.

Pooja was 'initially, very overwhelmed by the whole thing. When you don't know the person really well and somebody confides in you, it's a bit scary, but once I got to know how crazy and stupid and idiotic you are, I said, you're like me! And then there's no boundaries of friendship, you go all the way.'

Thankfully, and to the best of my knowledge, I haven't had friends who have betrayed my confidence—and I hope it wouldn't bother me even if they did.

As Bessel Van der Kolk, author of *The Body Keeps the Score*, writes, '. . . social support is not the same as merely being in the presence of others. The critical issue is reciprocity: being truly heard and seen by the people around us, feeling that we are held in someone else's mind and heart. For our physiology to calm down, heal, and grow we need a visceral feeling of safety. No doctor can write a prescription for friendship and love: these are complex and hard-earned capacities.' [1]

What's in it for the ally? That is a natural question. For many, the answer was simple: friendship. As Seema says, 'What other way is there to be a friend?'

Saumya elaborates on this sentiment. 'Being friends with someone who is bipolar is no different than any other friendship . . . you just accept it as part of who we are and don't see the mood swings as an "issue" in the friendship. It's important to remind yourself that your friend's bipolar disorder doesn't define them and you don't equate your friend with the disorder. I've been part of your mental health journey for over fifteen years. I would like to think that this journey has brought us closer as friends. I had accepted the symptoms early on. Solid friendships, such as ours, are one of the more stable and reassuring aspects of both our lives. Part of that friendship involves understanding how your symptoms may affect our bond and weathering those ups and downs.'

Friendships are, of course, built on reciprocity, as Van der Kolk says. 'You are a really loving person, you're unusually unselfish. And you're unusually giving of your time, your thoughts and everything. And that's very special,' says Shazia.

Mentors concur with the notion of friendship. 'Given my relationship with Amit and with your family, I felt happy to be useful, to be honest. What more can you offer in life than to be of some use to your friends?' says Rajeev. 'I won't even use the word "help". Just being around for each other. Not out of formality or courtesy, only strong bonding,' Sanjayji believes.

Khozem says he gets 'an awful lot. I've come to realize I really like and derive a great pleasure from bringing people and ideas together, showing people that actually it is possible to hop, skip and jump from here, and land somewhere there'. He once offered me a very interesting potential job opportunity in publishing, which I couldn't eventually pursue due to existing family commitments. 'I do genuinely like putting an opportunity in front of people. Even if those people, like you, have come from a privileged background, but they don't necessarily have opportunities in areas of their choosing. I felt you needed intelligent encouragement, not just sentimental encouragement.'

The third type of allies are networks, such as my Bombay Feminist Book Club and my writers' group. The word 'network' underestimates just how much these special groups have helped me evolve as a writer and channel my creative energies.

February 2015, Mumbai

It is early evening. I am sitting in the balcony of my home in Mumbai with Marona, a Dutch friend from my book club. A few days earlier, we discussed An Unquiet Mind *in the book club, and I had shared some of my writing on being bipolar with them. The feedback was unequivocal—do more!*

Marona and I decide to continue the conversation and she comes over. She is the first person with whom I share my vision for the book—how I want to write a memoir that includes the perspectives of my family, my medical practitioners and more. 'You seem pretty determined, I think you can do it,' she says. Her encouragement leads me to the start line of this marathon. My book is born.

The Bombay Feminist Book Club, started in 2012 by Mary, an American expat, is a small group of women who read books by, of and about women. The club meets every six weeks to discuss a particular text. The discussions are nuanced and in-depth, and each member loves reading. This is why I thought it would be the perfect space to discuss my dream of writing this book—for honest, unbiased critique, as well as nurturing support. And that's exactly what I received.

'You had this group of relative, not strangers, but not intimate friends, certainly. And so I think that that had a certain freedom to it, that you could sort of bring a different aspect of yourself to that setting, than you would to your normal social circle. Maybe half of the group was expats, for a while. And there also could have been the fact that mental health may be more openly talked about in the West than it was, at least at the time, in India. And we were critically engaging with women's roles in society as part of our discussion of books. I feel like that raised a lot of questions for all of us about our own roles as members of our families and mothers and sisters and daughters. I would say it was a progressive group in that way,' observes Mary, who has now relocated out of Mumbai.

It became a safe space to share feelings as well as writing. On one occasion, I felt like one of my medical practitioners was being patronizing, undermining my writing ambitions. Upset, I formed a WhatsApp group with those in the book club I was closest to, sharing my exasperation. The group immediately responded with supportive comments. One member, who says she likes to fight challenges with humour, even came up with some memorable feminist memes to lighten the mood.

Another member Hema notices that, 'when you enjoy anything, whether it's a yoga class with a very small group you've had an intimate journey with or whether it's a book club like ours, you have a journey with them, which is far more holistic. That holistic aspect plays a huge role in informing the larger brain, the larger background, the larger plane of your mental health'.

What the book club started, my writers' group is completing. Started by Sonya, an author, journalist and avid reader, the group comprises a mix of writers from across genres. We meet to discuss one another's work, do writing exercises, hear from other writers and, in my case, read many drafts of my manuscript.

'This group of listeners is sympathetic, empathetic and also analytical. They have been exposed to a lot of writing, they've read a lot and they know the pitfalls of trying to tell a story. A lot of it may be in your head and you may not necessarily know how to translate it on to paper, how you need to put in certain dialogue or make it more immediate to capture different voices. So they've struggled with these problems themselves. And they are in a good place to give you constructive advice,' says Sonya.

Mentors, friends, networks—this looks like dozens of allies to count on during a crisis. This is what political scientist Robert Putnam calls 'social capital' or 'networks, norms, and social trust that facilitate coordination and cooperation for mutual benefit. For a variety of reasons, life is easier in a community blessed with a substantial stock of social capital' in a seminal paper, 'Bowling Alone: America's Declining Social Capital.'[2]

But the important point to note is that I didn't first approach these individuals during a crisis. The crisis was preceded by solid friendships and relationships—by trusting them with my vulnerability, by my willingness to confide in them and to be a good friend myself. In other words, by investing in social capital all my life.

Robert Waldinger, a psychiatrist and a professor at Harvard Medical School, speaks about the value of relationships in a 2015 TED Talk that has been viewed over 20 million times on YouTube. He cites a seventy-five-year-old, ongoing Harvard study on happiness, which examines two groups of men, across generations, in Boston: the affluent and not-so-affluent.[3]

'The clearest message that we get from this seventy-five-year study is this: good relationships keep us happier and healthier. Period. We've learned three big lessons about relationships,' he says. [4]

First, 'it turns out that people who are more socially connected to family, to friends, to community, are happier, they're physically healthier and they live longer than people who are less well connected. And the experience of loneliness turns out to be toxic'.[5]

Second, 'it is not the number of friends that you have, and it's not whether or not you're in a committed relationship, but it's the quality of your close relationships that matters'.[6]

And finally, 'good relations don't just protect our bodies, they protect our brains. It turns out that being in a securely attached relationship with another person in your eighties is protective, that the people who are in relationships where they really feel that they can count on the other person in times of need, those people's memories stay sharper and longer'.[7]

In other words, 'the good life is built with good relationships'.[8]

Amen to that. I cannot overestimate how important my relationships with my allies are to my mental and emotional health.

There are increasingly new spaces where one can locate allies. For example, Daniel Lobo's BecauseYOU, a social enterprise that is creating a community for people dealing with mental health issues. Affected with bipolar disorder himself, Daniel founded BecauseYOU to 'bring the power of community and a journey of self-discovery together— to create a safe, aspirational space for people impacted by mental health issues. Our vision is to create an ecosystem of support for the person dealing with a mental health issue'.

'An individual enters the community through the essentials programme (five sessions, ninety minutes each), that's focused on reflection, coping skills and building a sense of comfort with group-based work. Each group is held by two facilitators—one trained psychotherapist and another who has a lived experience of a mental health issue. After this programme, the individual has access to support group sessions, workshops by experts, a private BecauseYOU social network and other tailored programmes. We believe that working in groups and creating safe spaces have a massive impact on a person's journey. Our work is not a replacement for individual therapy, but complementary,' says Daniel.

The for-profit business is 'mission-driven and aimed at the middle- and upper-middle-class segment at the moment,' he says. Participants are usually in the age range of twenty-three to thirty-five, from across India and some NRIs around the world.

'I love being part of the BecauseYOU community, it's a source of comfort for me. The facilitators truly "get it" since they have been on the journey themselves. I find that I am able to connect better to the people outside the community, by practising vulnerability within the community,' testifies one member.

* * *

I would like to end with a poem on friendship, composed a few years ago during a phase of extended stability.

The Festive Season

WhatsApp has turned friendship into a radio station
Turn on, tune in, switch off
Or maybe a low-flying drone
Hovering in the background

Facebook has turned friendship into a metric
Of names and numbers
Do our scores really matter?

Cocktail parties have turned friendship into a carousel
Where we circle around a buffet
Neither talking nor eating
Just inquiring—so, what do you do?

So let's say thanks to old-fashioned dining tables
Striped, round or asymmetric

Where only as many friends meet
As there are seats.
For conversations, jokes and sometimes confessions

And home-cooked food
—by anyone other than me.

What I'm realizing is that I can only have the professional (and personal) success I want if I am able to break out of the **Vicious Cycle of Bipolarity:**

Grandiose plans → great expectations → short time lines → stress & excitement → lack of sleep → escapism → fantasy/delusion → mania → lack of success → depression → need for affirmation → grandiose projects.

Instead, I need to adopt a Virtuous Cycle of Fulfilment:

Step-by-step plan → measured pace → consistent, incremental feedback → balanced lifestyle with diverse projects → steady milestones → ongoing success → new step-by-step plan

Writing it down doesn't come naturally to me, forget following it, but this is what I will really need to do. If I'm not stable, I will not be able to get the kind of success I want. So it's the opposite: aim for success by not aiming for it, and focusing on small actions, rather than outcomes.

19 October 2016
(extract from journal)

7

Work Therapy and Playing Opposite-Handed

January 2013, Mumbai

I am at my desk in my bedroom in Mumbai and my mind is in a tailspin. Back from the ashram in Bihar, I am disappointing not one, not two, not three, but four editors at the Mint at the same time.

My most ambitious writing, a series of seven back-to-back, full-page stories on Indian urbanization, commissioned by Mint's editor-in-chief R. Sukumar, is in jeopardy. One of the longest series by a single byline, it has even been pre-advertised in the paper. For months, I have travelled around the country, doing dozens of interviews.

But now I am filing stories late, painting my editors into a corner. I forget to take a photographer with me during my travels, which makes photoshoots more cumbersome. Even though I somehow manage to write my stories and the series is well-received, when I ask one of Mint's senior editors, Anil, for feedback on the series (and another writing opportunity) he says: 'We've decided not to give such a long series to a single reporter.'

A parallel interview with a senior urban thinker, visiting from New York, is also bungled. My editor Niranjan and I meet this academic at a hotel in south Mumbai. I am ready with my tape recorder, but for the first time in my journalistic career, I am not mindful enough to record it properly. I come home and am devastated to see that I have only eleven minutes recorded of an hour-long conversation. Of course, I am not coherent enough to recall what was said. When I recover a few weeks later, I email the academic some follow-up questions and he is kind enough to reply with detailed answers. But it is too late to print the story.

And I miss deadlines for my regular column, 'Head Office', letting down Seema Chowdhry, my immediate editor and boss, who is also based in Delhi. Between January and April 2013, the monthly column, which I am contractually obliged to file, is irregular, partly because I had been occupied with the urbanization series and partly because I am unwell for most of January and February. The column appears as a double-page centre spread at the time, so its absence is visible.

I feel like a total failure.

I failed at the family business—and was asked to leave it.

I have failed at being a journalist—doing a job I loved.

I am crushed; depressed for several months.

And now I have to tell my boss that I am bipolar.

● ● ●

A sense of awkwardness hovered over me in early 2013 when I called Seema Chowdhry to tell her that I was bipolar. Amit had already informed her that I needed some time off and asked her for her support, without specifying the nature of the problem. He conveyed that I remained very interested in what I do but that I wasn't in a position to answer emails or phone calls. Seema says she didn't inquire further and gave me the space I sought.

'You were very sheepish. You said, "sometimes I have these episodes". That's when you told me you had bipolar disorder. I didn't know what it was then, I looked it up. I remember thinking to myself, "but I've never experienced it". I mean the way you presented yourself, I never thought that it existed with you. But then I also realized that most of my connection with you at that point in time was on the phone or email,' Seema says.

Telling your boss that you're bipolar is not the easiest conversation, especially when you've been behind on work, but it helped our relationship. 'I don't know if you felt it, but I think after that conversation my attitude towards your work, and towards you, also changed quite a bit. One of the things that I realized in that period was that if people are honest about their issue, or about the circumstances that they are in, then it's easier for the person opposite to empathize and make an effort to understand. Maybe I didn't know the details but at least I could change the way I behaved with you. Before I found out that this was a problem, I would get frustrated, I didn't know what was happening. Once I came to know that this is an issue, when the next deadline was not met, I was prepared for it. I don't think I suddenly became an empathetic person or I was making allowances out of the blue, I'm not trying to project that. But I did understand mental illness-related issues better than a lot of other people, because I've lived with a more severe form of it, with a mentally challenged sibling. So it was easier for me to accept it,' Seema explains.

Over the course of a decade, Seema and I were able to create a niche in writing on business and design that didn't previously exist, as the column gained popularity and established itself as a regular fixture in the paper. It evolved from being a column on CEOs' workspaces and workstyles to a column on leadership, business and design, leading to a book, released by Penguin Random House India.

15 September 2015: The Four Seasons Hotel, Mumbai

I am conducting rapid-fire questions on design and business to a panel of CEOs, including N. Chandrasekaran, then the CEO of Tata Consultancy Services, Shikha Sharma, formerly of Axis Bank, my uncle Ajay Piramal of the Piramal Group and Amar Goel of PubMatic. We go back and forth, with shared rapport and repartee, and the audience laughs at our camaraderie. About 300 people are seated inside the banquet hall; there are over 100 mingling outside who couldn't get into the room. The head of the Asia Society India Centre, our partner for the launch, asks us to untie ribbons as we unveil the book. A representative from Penguin introduces it. Seema delivers the closing remarks. My first book, Working Out of the Box: 40 Stories of Leading CEOs, *is officially launched. It is a major professional milestone.*

Seema and I became closer, and a few years later, she sent me a couple of handwritten notes, which I have preserved because they are so special to me:

6.12.2017

Dear Aparna,
I don't say this often and enough number of times but thank you for being a columnist with me, for believing in my vision and making it your own, then bringing so much amazing energy to it that now it's all yours totally. Lots of love, Seema.

And another one, just before she left the *Mint*, for an opportunity in education:

29.03.2019:

Dear Aparna,
A decade together . . . well we went from being colleagues to becoming friends. Thank you for listening to me, thank you for being enthusiastic about your column and about *Mint* at large. Sometimes I shot down your ideas, sometimes I sensed your frustration, but as your editor I had to keep a view of the larger page in mind. Anyway, I am really going to miss working with you. I will always cherish our interactions. Lots of love, Seema.

I soon discovered that sharing my condition with my other colleagues was just as helpful in enhancing our working relationship. For example, I realized that Sukumar was prepared to overlook the messy processes of the 2012 urban series and grant me another opportunity—to interview a group of global thinkers who were gathering in Delhi for an urban conference in late 2014. Once again, back-to-back full-page stories. This time, when he handed me what seemed to be a tight deadline, I explained my condition and asked for an extension. It was given.

Sukumar says he thought my previous work was 'authoritative and had expertise' and warranted leeway. 'If you are sure that someone has a condition and you are aware of it, you can make allowances for it. I always make allowances for good workers if someone's work is going to be really top-notch. I was more than happy to give you the second job,' he says. Although I did in fact take a bit longer than anticipated to file my stories, the urban thinker series ran in early 2015 and did well for the paper.

By 2017, bipolarity was part of my official resume. When higher education pioneer Pramath Raj Sinha asked me to teach as a visiting faculty member at the Anant National University in Ahmedabad, I issued the statutory warning: 'I'm bipolar and there may be an incident which might disrupt my ability to teach or to adhere to the teaching schedule.'

'Thanks for letting me know,' he said. There was indeed an incident six months later, where I had taken on too many projects, was hypomanic and unable to teach but he was able to react with understanding, and I was taken off the teaching programme and subsequently reinstated with a suitable break.

It is wonderful to be so comfortable in your skin that you reach the stage when it doesn't matter. When I asked my current features editors at the *Mint*, Delhi-based Shalini Umachandran and Pooja Singh, for an interview to discuss my upcoming book on mental health, they issued one-line replies:

'To be perfectly honest, I didn't know you had a mental health condition at all.'

'Had you not told me, I wouldn't have known.'

I had reached the point of stability where I had forgotten to mention it to them. I only hope it stays that way.

◉ ◉ ◉

This chapter would be incomplete without a reference to a period in my professional life about which I am very nostalgic: my time as the head of BP Ergo, my family's office furniture business. As mentioned earlier, I ran this business from 2002 to 2005, before its sale, as its COO.

Yes, chief operating officer, but also as I like to joke, Child Of Owner!

If I was COO, Ergo was my baby and I wanted to nurture it as such. I was in my twenties and it was my first experience of general management and leadership. Although I subsequently moved to writing as a profession, my time at Ergo was very special. When I took over, the company made a minor loss, but when I left, it was resolutely profitable. During this time, we improved financials, expanded headcount and scope of operations, acquired a new corporate identity, strengthened the brand and enhanced its competitive positioning—as acknowledged by our competitors and customers. Yes, the market moved in our favour but I like to think we were able to maximize the opportunities facing us. From being the first Indian office furniture company to exhibit our products at a major international exhibition to handling some of the most complicated workplace fit-outs in the country, we were ready to innovate and take on challenges.

Interestingly, during this time I was largely stable, apart from a small bout of hypomania in 2003. There were times initially when I was worried about the business but I do not remember losing sleep. I attribute this to my desire to work independently, supported by a great team.

To understand what I was like as a colleague and as a boss, I spoke to some of my former colleagues—Alok, then head of sales, Nitin, then head of manufacturing, Manoj, then head of human resources, and Ranjit, then head of marketing.

Most of them did not encounter visible symptoms of bipolarity. As Ranjit says, 'You were in the office, you were there late in the evening and you were actively engaged in doing something. You were perfectly normal.' Nitin did remark that my moods could vary to some extent. 'You could be a little scary. There used to be a fear that you might suddenly erupt, I had to be cautious before approaching you and be very sure with numbers, language, grammar. But sometimes you used to be so nice that one would wonder whether it is the same Aparna I remembered of yesterday or last fortnight. When you were in an agitated mood, it was completely different,' he says.

Manoj noticed my energy on some occasions but it never rose to worrying levels. 'Sometimes your energy was remarkable. You used to work all day at the factory and then we would continue to work back at the hotel and you'd be at the factory at 9 a.m. the next day. You became far more creative than the normal course, getting into the minor details of all activities.'

I see it as a period when I channelled passion with intellect—mostly productively, and maybe a little too obsessively at times. Which is not to say there wasn't scepticism of my ambitions—even though they didn't doubt the direction I was steering the company in, my former colleagues often wondered if my ideas could be implemented in the time frame I had suggested.

Yet looking back, their comments on other aspects of my leadership style are gratifying. 'As a senior leader, you need two things. You need freedom to work and second, you need direction, and if these two things are balanced, it goes fine. I used to get insights from you about what should be the role of manufacturing, in terms of lifting the brand, in terms of quality, in terms of design, which I implemented. And I got ample freedom. It was a very nice blend, which is what made the best of me,' says Nitin. 'Honestly, it was the best time I had in my career ever,' states Alok.

More importantly, the team still bonds, as Alok points out to me. Beyond the active WhatsApp group, 'the team still chats with each other, talks to each other. A lot of them work with each other now. Some got married to each other. The sense of teamwork really happened for us'. Which is great. Finally, most of my former colleagues have grown and flourished in new roles as they progressed beyond the company, expanding their area of expertise.

I share this story to exemplify two ideas—first, that although work can be stressful, it can also be therapeutic. Being productive can make you happy. And second, that you can be in a leadership position, family business or not, whilst living with a mental health condition. As Alok says, 'You were not just pulling along, you were actually leading. If you're passionate about something, and serious about it, maybe all other problems become secondary, your passion virtually takes over your life.'

The challenge is to locate the right bandwidth—too much work makes me stressed, too little work makes me depressed. My range of bandwidth is thus narrower than most. As I wrote in my diary on 7 November 2013:

Avoid episodes by avoiding stress: My self-image is of someone who can handle a lot. So when I take on too many projects and can't handle, I think I slip into a fantasy world where I can handle a lot.

To exist within my bandwidth, I have devised a metaphor called 'playing opposite-handed'—learning to work as if you were playing a sport with your opposite hand: slower, more mindfully, with more breaks between shots. This might seem unnatural at first but I find it is more sustainable. I conceived of this idea back in 2016 and this is what I wrote in my journal. It remains one of the important lessons over the last twenty years of being bipolar.

27 September 2016

This note looks at the mechanics of the process that leads me to the high, in an attempt to cope with them. For example, after a very encouraging meeting with a potential publisher about my book, I found myself pressurizing myself with deadlines—could I complete the manuscript in three months? How many words would I need to write every day? How many have I written already? How soon should I send her a chapter?

And then I found myself getting a little freaked out at having potentially bitten off more than I could chew: Would I really have the guts to have this published? Would I be able to persuade my family to come on board? Could I really see myself on a TV show? Could I be a public figure on the topic? Have I got sufficient distance and detachment from the emotions surrounding the material that I could even write the book? And inevitably, the combination of fear and anxiety led me to lose sleep, and I had to take a sedative to go to bed.

Luckily, I was not manic, and I realized that if I continue to stress myself, this project would have to be shelved, which would devastate me. I decided instead to visit my counsellor Suneeta Mehta and discuss it. She explained that I'm still fragile from the last episode, and my brain needs a rest from over-stimulating material, and I appreciated her non-judgemental tone of voice.

There was an important realization: I need to learn how to play left-handed. In other words, I need to adopt the opposite behaviour of my natural instincts if I want to cope with bipolarity without sacrificing my ambitions.

My natural pattern when approaching a professional challenge is to make grandiose plans and look for quick results, achieved through intense activity, resulting in fear, stress and excitement all at once. This makes me lose sleep, I feel helpless, seek escapism and plunge into an alternative reality, ultimately resulting in mania.

That is playing right-handed, that is what comes naturally to me.

So should I stop playing cricket (or table tennis in my case) and give up all my hopes and dreams? That's what a well-meaning psychiatrist would say. But I think he/she would be wrong.

I need to learn how to bat left-handed—or play opposite-handed. Another way of putting it:

The mind is a wild horse, chafing at the bit for more intellectual stimulation, for a spurt of gallop. It feels it is destined to do so, and that no other alternative exists.

Reining it in is not deprivation, even though the wild horse may feel like it is being thwarted of its destiny and purpose.

Slow down to appreciate the unhurried symmetry of the trot or even the patient drumbeat of the walk.

There will still be fences to jump, mountains to climb, where the horse is exercised and challenged, *where it will do much better if the intellect is in charge, rather than just the emotion.* Where ambition and intellect can coexist, without stress, fear or adrenaline.

The sharpest intellect is the well-rested one.

And yes, don't stop riding—that's (almost) the worst advice you can get.

In other words, accept that nothing that is worth having happens quickly. Grandiose plans needn't be jettisoned altogether, but they need focus, resilience and patience.

Playing opposite-handed also means savouring the 'joy of creation', taking time to enjoy the nuance of creation as much as its grandeur. It means not needing as much external validation, because slow craftsmanship generates intrinsic satisfaction. Playing opposite-handed might require hitting slower and deeper, rather than faster and shallower, and it might take longer to make a mark, but it is better than knocking yourself out in the first over.

I need to teach myself to play opposite-handed. It is not what comes naturally, but for me, it might be the only way to negotiate the friction between my chemical khichdi, my hopes and my reality.

Playing opposite-handed has become the bedrock of my approach to work. I pursue many activities, but only a little bit at a time. I write a column, but it's monthly, not weekly. I teach a class, but it's only for a month in a year. I advise a start-up and a non-profit, but part-time. I write books, but only one every few years. There's always more I want to do, but on most days, there's more than enough time for a short afternoon nap!

● ● ●

There are lessons for employers too. My bosses, colleagues, mentors and friends offered me their first-hand takeaways from past instances of managing employees with mental health challenges.

Attitude to mental health appears to be foremost in shaping reactions. 'It's not that I've had a lot of experience, but I have somewhere got it in my head that mental illness is like heart disease or diabetes or endometriosis or joint pain that comes and goes, and people live with it. And there are phases when it's bad, and there are phases when it's okay,' acknowledges Pramath.

Sukumar realizes that companies need to adapt to a varied workforce. 'This is not a Frederick Winslow Taylorian, industrial management kind of thing where you expect everyone to wear uniforms, to come in to work and work exactly the same way at the same pace, deliver the same quality of work. Once you acknowledge that, and once you're willing to invest time and effort in getting the best out of people, different people might need different kinds of allowances. Someone might be bipolar, someone might have Asperger's, someone might have ADHD.* Someone might be dyslexic, but otherwise a great worker. How the newsroom uses them is up to the newsroom and up to the manager.'

One of my mentors, Luis, admits that his attitude has changed over time. 'I must confess that when I was working for the first twenty-odd years in banking and in private equity, one wasn't exposed to this that much. It's only in the last ten years when I've actually quit full-time work that I'm more aware of these situations. My attitude in those days was these are all excuses. So it's very possible that I could have

---

* According to the American Psychological Association, 'ADHD, or attention-deficit/hyperactivity disorder, is a behavioral condition that makes focusing on everyday requests and routines challenging. People with ADHD typically have trouble getting organized, staying focused, making realistic plans, and thinking before acting. They may be fidgety, noisy, and unable to adapt to changing situations.'

had people on our team who may have had mental health challenges that, frankly, I didn't understand or appreciate.

'Today, I'm hearing a lot more people, in the organizations that I'm involved with, talking about some of their challenges. For example, there's one person I was talking to who told me how he hasn't slept for the last one month, how he's taking sleeping pills for the first time in his life. I looked back and thought, I've never had this type of a conversation in those twenty years that I was in banking or in private equity. So, maybe it is just people are more aware that there are challenges and, therefore, they need to do something about it and are more honest about it.'

A willingness to free the unwell person from immediate responsibilities and commitments is vital, without them losing their place in the organization, as Pramath did with my teaching schedule. He also likes to make sure that anyone undergoing a mental health challenge 'is connected to people, and not isolated. Whether it's friends or family with their permission, because I know that's an issue also sometimes'.

Getting professional help is the next—and obvious—step, in the form of a counsellor or a mental health practitioner. Pramath has partnered with tech-based counsellors YourDost in 'every campus. That's how I started to come to terms with the fact that this was actually almost becoming an epidemic'.

Seema spoke to me about a former colleague who was suicidal. She took the colleague to a psychologist for two months. Sukumar was very supportive, saying that either the company would pay for the treatment or that insurance would reimburse the expenses.

At the same time, empathy should not translate into pity. 'They shouldn't be seen as "poor things". I don't think most organizations today would sack a person because of mental illness. But sometimes that person becomes an object of pity. I don't think that is very helpful either. Even though I went through a month of panic attacks and had to seek psychiatric help, my editors at that point of time were quite supportive,' says a senior journalist friend.

In the long run, companies can establish specific practices to promote mental health. For example, finding the right fit between employee and employer is the beginning in promoting a harmonious working relationship.

'If someone reacts very badly to stress, you can't have them in certain functions that are time-related or deadline-related, but at the same time it is possible to accommodate them in places where time and deadlines are not all that important. The most important thing to my mind is that you need to have managers who recognize the fact that people have an issue and are willing to accommodate those issues, and that usually happens when the worker is otherwise very good at what he or she does,' observes Sukumar.

One of my mentors, investment banker Rajeev, is frank about the challenges in balancing an employee's aspirations with his capabilities and his mental health. 'We have had people who are not able to handle the stress of the job, not able to work with the timelines or not able to handle a difficult, demanding client. We have one such young professional who's got a very good mind but he can't handle the stress. He says he likes the job very much. But every now and then he puts his phone off, he's not accessible. You try to reach him in many, multiple ways. And then you get a call from his wife saying, "he is in very bad shape". I just don't know how to handle him. To be honest with you, I don't know what to do. He's in the wrong profession; he needs to be in a commercial banking role which has different processes,' Rajeev points out.

I can empathize with the young man. As I said in chapter one, my only experience of working in an investment bank, as a summer intern in New York, was a disaster because I couldn't handle the deadline-driven work environment. Sometimes one just has to accept it's not the best fit.

My college friend Alok, who is now a partner with a global consulting firm, says that his firm offers a 'full and complete set of support services from access to qualified therapists, health and wellness programmes, peer learning, including on meditation and other techniques, to supporting leave and time off with no questions. We have official policies and programmes in place where you can take a pause. It's called "My Time". You can just say, "I'm going to take the next two months off", with no consequences whatsoever. You don't have to explain to someone what you're doing with your time off, whether it's meeting your grandparents or pursuing a hobby or rejuvenating your mental health or anything else.

'And similarly, we have a lot of professional help. We have an anonymous ombudsperson that you can talk to as well. If someone says, "Look, I don't want to talk to my professional development person or HR person in the office", those mental health resources are available, even if you were to ask anonymously. So we've tried to create a lot of different support systems. We call it emotional well-being and believe strongly that your emotional well-being is as important as your professional success,' he says.

It is not just about those with mental health conditions; employers of caregivers need to be mindful of mental health too, as mental illness affects caregivers' abilities to work. 'In the National Mental Health Survey, it was observed that family members had to forego [sic] on an average 10 working days in the previous 3 months to take care of those with chronic conditions like schizophrenia, other psychotic disorders and bipolar affective disorder,' says the NIMHANS report.[1]

Amit worked in the private equity team of global financial services major Goldman Sachs for nearly a decade, from 2012 to 2020, during which time I experienced most of my ups and downs. It was a regional office with a small team, headed then by a senior partner, Ankur Sahu. Amit says his colleagues 'were very supportive during those troubled times', giving him flexibility to be with the children when needed and letting him catch up on work after they went to bed.

'Amit and I had a strong and trusted relationship, and we worked closely together on many things. It was pretty clear that something was going on. Initially he wouldn't be that open but then he told me what he was going through. From my perspective, family is always number one. I told him, "you don't even have to take leave, you just do what you have to do to take care of things at home. And we can manage the work amongst the team." I think that's kind of how we made it through that. My priority is always to focus on getting the job done, it doesn't matter whether you do it from Hawaii or from Bombay,' says Ankur.

Junior team members, such as Ridhi Chaudhry, also came through. 'Amit and I overlapped for six years. I got to know about this after a few years, not from day one. He told me about something that was going on in his mind. He's always been calm and composed, he never lost that, but he generally became a little quiet and a bit isolated during those times. I just listened patiently and made sure I did as much as possible to cover for him at work, whenever he wanted to spend more time at home to deal with the situation.'

Both Ankur and Ridhi reinforced that just as there has been progress on other aspects of diversity and inclusion in

companies—whether gender, race or sexuality—there needs
to be equivalent awareness and sensitivity to mental health
and wellness in the workplace.

Richard Friedman, chairman of the asset management
division of Goldman Sachs and then Amit's ultimate boss
based in New York, is a pioneer in this field. 'Once, when I
visited New York, Rich told me about his association with
Mount Sinai Hospital in New York and how he was funding
neurological research through the Friedman Brain Institute.
I told Rich about your illness and he offered to support me
with introductions in New York. I will always be thankful to
Rich as during every trip he used to enquire about you and
your health,' Amit says.

These are examples of progressive employers, but the truth
is that the workplace remains a stressful and depressing place
for many, and ill-equipped to manage mental health challenges.

'Many companies are finally talking about mental
health at work but leaders and managers are slow to
change the work part of it although the major workplace
stressors, which have been known for decades, have been
made worse by Covid-19. Leaders and managers should be
asking: "What changes can we make in the way we manage,
and our company responds to our depressed, anxious new
normal? How do you reward the individual at work, not just
financially?" Because piling on deliverables as if nothing
had changed while encouraging self-care and yoga can feel
a bit like being told to take swim classes to improve your
stroke—when you are drowning,' argues Carin-Isabel
Knoop, author of *Compassionate Management of Mental Health
in the Modern Workplace.* 'Workplace stressors include
excessive or insufficient workload; lack of participation and
control; monotonous or unpleasant tasks; role ambiguity
or conflict; lack of recognition; inequity; poor interpersonal

relationships; poor working conditions; poor leadership and communication; and conflicting home and work demands,'[2] she says, citing a WHO report on workplace mental health. Research validates her perspective: 'Of 1.2 million active registered companies in India, only 1000 provide structured services for mental health to their employees,' says 'All in the Mind: The State of Mental Health in Corporate India.'[3]

Amit Malik is a psychiatrist, a mental health entrepreneur and the founder of InnerHour, a mental health platform. 'Surveys suggest that one in two people are experiencing significant levels of psychological morbidity in terms of stress, anxiety and depressive illnesses in the Indian corporate workforce. That number is quite high,' he states. InnerHour offers evidence-based, data-led structured interventions in the form of comprehensive, customized programmes with multiple touchpoints—assessments, workshops, webinars, corporate communications, access to therapists and a self-care app.

'Depression, relationship difficulties both at work and at home, and addictions are three big areas that people really seek our help for in the corporate world. And the underlying work-related risk factors include poor work-life balance, lack of connection to purpose of work and lack of understanding of where I fit in the larger organization,' he says.

Covid-19 has exponentially increased the need. 'We have grown three–four times in terms of the number of monthly downloads, in corporate employees served, in revenue, in the last year. I do feel that there's been a step change in the corporate workforce in terms of how mental health is viewed in the last year. Even traditional organizations that would not have been that open to talking about it, or even creating environments that are conducive to conversation, have now come out and said, "let's do something about this". When leaders start talking about mental health difficulties, it encourages people to have more open conversations and seek out help. We've seen engagement also go up in the past year,' he says.

Nalini Saligram is another change-maker offering hope. Her non-profit, Arogya World, seeks to prevent non-communicable diseases through 'health education and lifestyle change'. Their flagship workplace programme is their Healthy Workplace initiative, which in 2021 for the first time included mental health as a mandatory criterion alongside existing physical health and non-communicable disease prevention criteria (such as healthy eating, a no-tobacco policy and physical activity). About 150 companies spanning more than 3.1 million employees have been recognized by the non-profit as 'Healthy Workplaces' at their annual conference and awards events.

Saligram says that their clients prompted them to include mental health criteria during the Covid-19 lockdown. 'We were doing a lot of webinars during this time. HR managers and business leaders said to us "tell me what I should do to take care of the emotional health and mental health of my employees, when they're so stressed, living and working from home. I need to do something, but I don't know where to start. Give us a blueprint," they said.'

Arogya World partnered with global mental health experts to help devise a set of values- and evidence-based criteria, launched in November 2020, that were merged with Arogya's physical health criteria. The criteria, which are accessible on the NGO's website, include 'Promote Well-Being, Managing Stress, Leadership and Supporting Recovery'. Companies are awarded bronze, silver or gold after an assessment, depending on how many points they earn. More partnerships with industry associations makes Arogya World optimistic of being a workplace mental health pioneer in India.

'Companies find it particularly challenging to gain acceptance for mental health programmes among the workforce. Even though many leaders have a good understanding of mental health issues at the workplace, it's still a difficult topic to raise in the workplace. People do not talk openly about mental health at work since they are afraid of being labelled as mentally ill and afraid that they may lose their jobs. Senior leaders do not openly talk about their own issues with the result that employees remain silent,' observes Saligram.

I hope very much that Arogya World is able to ignite a movement to counter this predicament. Poor mental health has a staggering impact on the economy. India stands to suffer a loss of $1.03 trillion (approximately Rs 77.25 lakh crore) in an eighteen-year period (2012 to 2030) due to mental health conditions alone,[4] reports 'Economics of Non-Communicable Diseases in India: The Costs and Returns on Investment of Interventions to Promote Healthy Living and Prevent, Treat, and Manage NCDs' by the World Economic Forum and the Harvard School of Public Health.

I would like to end with a poem I wrote after leaving the family business. I found myself on long train rides on summer expeditions with the children, taking them beyond central London. The poem reminds me of the idea of 'playing opposite-handed'.

Gentle

I emerged from my years-long cocoon
Of motherhood and parenting
And found myself on a train
A slow train

A train?
What was I doing here?
I only boarded planes earlier
And here I am on a slow train
Did I really wear suits before I boarded the slow train?
Do there have to be many more stops on the slow train?

Then I realize
It's not pace that separates fast and slow trains
It's not speed, or purpose, or direction
The difference is simply: one's gentler on me

Gentle is a way of being
Tolerating tele-marketeers
Holding your child's hand, not dragging it
Sharing your work anxieties with your boss
Not hoarding or downloading on the husband

Gentle is the realization
That just because you do it every day,
It doesn't have to be a chore

Most of it, it's knowing that
The person who needs gentle most
Will always be me.
I'm the heart of my family.

So whichever train I decide to board,
Sometimes fast, sometimes slow,
It's only if I can get it to be
Just that little bit gentler on me.

I think I've managed to trace the root cause of my problems—internal conflict—and understood the consequences of not aligning "head, heart and hand" for me. I've only now understood how deeply it affects me. When I'm facing emotional turmoil, I let myself get stressed and descend into an "alternative reality". The question I need to ask myself now is: how will I handle such conflicts in the future? What can I do to align heart, head and mind?

December 2012

One of the highlights of the year for me was peaceful moments of solitude—chanting in the car, playing the piano, going for walks. Of course, I love being with people, especially friends, but if I have to think about what I enjoyed most about this year, it's about those moments of serenity I had to myself, they felt especially precious and significant.

20 December 2016
(extracts from journals)

8

Self-Therapy: Conversations on Identity, Purpose and Dharma

Mid-2003, Mumbai

My father dictates my resignation letter. I am twenty-seven years old, hypomanic, and he has lost confidence in my ability to lead our family's office furniture business as its executive director. Days pass, and I am determined to stay in the company. It is a huge part of my identity, my very being.

'Your behaviour had become very erratic and very rebellious. I was very worried that you might do something very stupid in the company and that is why I thought it would be safer to have your resignation to avoid any embarrassing eventuality,' said my father, years later.

I find a way back in. The resignation letter is not discussed—until I get married in 2004, move to London to accompany Amit, and my father asks me to resign from the board as I won't be in the country for some time. Once again, I am disappointed with the suggestion and continue to find ways to engage with the business.

March 2018, Mumbai

I stand on a small stage in the campus of the German School in Mumbai. Wearing a red kurta and trying not to trip over a pair of beige high heels, I deliver a ten-minute TEDx Talk on 'The Jungle Gym Career'. Inspired by the phrase in Sheryl Sandberg's book, Lean In, I describe how I moved from business to journalism—a sideways move, off the conventional corporate ladder. Our careers are like jungle gyms now, not a ladder, I reinforce, as we move in different directions.

I offer '3Ps' as tips to help navigate this new-age career: 'Pivot' with the help of mentors who can guide you through the twists and turns. Build up a 'Portfolio of activities' through networks of friends and associates. For example, I now write, teach, speak and give—all opportunities that came by through networks. 'Prototype' yourself, through experimenting with platforms—I talk about the initiatives that worked and those that didn't. I am confident, smiling and not disappointed when technical issues prevent the talk from being uploaded on YouTube. Just being able to distil and share my thoughts is enough.

A ten-minute talk that traversed fifteen years, this journey of professional transition is central to my bipolar story. Much changed in my personal life during this time—I acquired a husband, in-laws and became a mother. None of this impacted my sense of identity—and my mood swings—as much as my professional life.

As my business school classmate and close friend Samhita observes, 'I think professional validation and the ability to have the conversations that you have in your professional life with different people that you encounter through that realm is super important to you . . . your identity is very grounded in professional achievement, it's a very important piece of your self-worth and self-esteem. I don't think you would be happy without feeling fulfilled on that front. And that doesn't mean that you have to run some billion-dollar company, but you need to feel like you're around the sort of people you want to be around professionally, and that you're moving forward and making progress.'

She is right. I grew up with three defining beliefs related to myself and the world around me, based on the prevailing family business environment and my response to it: First, to be successful was to be an entrepreneur or businessperson, not just because of wealth and lifestyle, but because of standing, reputation, the lives at stake, contribution to society, assets at one's disposal . . . the general importance accorded to people of means, especially in a developing country. Second, that I was destined for this sort of success because of my intelligence, my family background and my willingness to work hard and third, that personal identity and professional success were closely linked, i.e., being successful meant being someone and vice versa. However naive or inflated they might sound, these were key tenets for my younger self.

I soon discovered, however, I wasn't necessarily cut out for the kind of professional success I had always taken for granted would come my way. This was for many reasons—my personality, my inclinations, family circumstances and considerations, and my mental and emotional health. I had to begin an 'inside-out shift'—to find a profession that suited my capabilities and interests, and I eventually landed on writing and journalism.

So how did I become an advocate for professional reinvention when it was something I previously feared and resisted? And how can this be relevant to others who may not be from a business family?

The changing nature of identity, purpose and meaning which dogged me for years is universal. Many of us, regardless of profession or career, struggle to find purpose or meaning in our lives—with or without a mental health condition. The lesson I have to offer, after so long, is singular. What matters, I believe, is the conversation you are having with yourself, the narrative you are framing of yourself, the story you tell yourself about who you are—your self-therapy. And it is a journey. I have tried to share it in detail just to show how relentless the self-questioning can be.

Three moments in time, in particular, set the stage for my self-therapy.

1. Mid-2012, Mumbai

I lie on the floor, wearing a T-shirt and track pants, in our living room in Mahim, watching my breath as my yoga teacher, Atmapadma, guides me in my practice. She is patient, warm and gentle. We finish our yoga session, and I begin talking with her about my move from my family business and my uncertain work life. And then she recites a single shloka from the Bhagavad Gita that changes my life. She does not delve into explanations but leaves me to meditate on it.

> *Better is one's dharma, even if imperfect*
> *Than another's dharma, followed perfectly*
> *Better is death in following one's own dharma,*
> *For another's dharma brings danger*[1]

(Chapter 3, Verse 35)

Many years later, she offers a commentary. 'For me personally, the lifelong search has been for truth, and to try and not just access it, but to live it. So therefore, on the question of dharma, the question is, be true to what? I can be true to being my father's daughter, I can be true to being a citizen of this country, I can be true to being the disciple of someone, there are so many roles that may come my way, or that I may choose to take on myself. When I read this shloka, and when I heard a bit about it, what I understood from it was that dharma is defined not as duty as we normally understand it to be (that it's your duty to fight as a warrior, for example) as much as wetness is the dharma of water and movement is the dharma of the wind. It is your essential nature. It is it what makes me who I am.

'When I'm doing that, which is close to my essential nature, I will come closer to peace. Whereas when I'm doing that which is alien to me, then you're not at ease, there is anxiety, there's a gap between the truth and what I'm trying to live as the truth,' she says.

She differentiates between the normal struggles that one may encounter in one's life journey when one tries to be true to one's path and the 'insecurities, fear, anxiety, neurosis and psychosis' that take place when one deviates from one's dharma.

'It's very elusive, because at different stages, what my dharma is in different situations, what my dharma is, is fluid sometimes. And it's very tricky to be alive to that something inside, rather than what has been defined by something outside,' she emphasizes.

My thoughts on the shloka make their way into my journal a few weeks after Atmapadma first recited the shloka:

I've been dwelling a lot on this shloka, and at the risk of sounding clichéd, weighing what it means to "have a life well-spent". It has left me with the following realizations:

I need to still find a way of turning my intellectual interests—writing, film, design—into something that is of value and will also fulfil my need of winning peer respect. This is both exciting—because there are several options, and the road is entirely open—as well as terrifying, because of the uncertainty.

I suspect that when I think of myself as a promoter's child or inheritor, I pressure myself to achieve a lot within a short span of time, or equally, get carried away by my own "credentials" and "position". I feel validated and affirmed, think of myself as an achiever, because this is what society expects of me.

However, when I think of myself as a writer/thinker, there's far more emphasis on the means, rather than just the ends. The journey is about the pursuit of excellence, of competing with oneself, of producing good work: perhaps that is something that ties in better with my personality, its strengths and its weaknesses. There is much less affirmation, the territory is unknown, and consequently the possibility of not being a super-achiever is sky-high. But it's intellectually richer, and more honest. Perhaps that is something which works better for me? What is the narrative of my life that I'm comfortable with? And will finding the answer to this prevent these "manic" episodes?

This was the beginning of a long line of journal entries on the subject of identity, dharma and purpose.

2. Mid-2015, Mumbai

Tara Mahadevan, a counselling psychologist, is dictating a few lines to me. We are seated next to each other in her home in Colaba. At the time, Tara specializes in mindful eating, in helping her clients understand why they eat what they eat. In addition to a 'food and water' plan aimed at weight loss, she presents me with a set of affirmations.

> *May I be free from stress and anxiety*
> *May I be at ease and balanced*
> *May I be happy*
> *May I be free from my past*
> *May I accept and choose myself the way I am because I am good enough*
> *May I move towards the light always*
> *May I be happy and fulfilled*

I write them down on index cards and store them carefully in my handbag. They accompany me wherever I go, to this day. She makes me set a reminder on my phone to say them to myself, at 6 p.m. every day (The reminder still exists, even though the ritual may have lapsed after the first year or so).

Not feeling good enough pervaded every cell of my brain, even though it may only have been visible to perceptive friends such as Tara. Coming from a family of high-achievers and having studied at elite educational institutes, I never felt that my 'achievements' were enough—especially given my mental illness. The combination of excessive ambition and heightened inadequacy, whilst probably familiar to many CEOs, is not a recommended recipe for arriving at emotional and mental balance.

For Tara, affirmations were vital to my well-being (I will write on mindful eating, which is equally critical, in more detail in the chapter on lifestyle therapy). 'Affirmations are a really effective way to rewire ourselves. The way the brain functions, or the way it's designed, is that the more we tell ourselves something, the more we believe it to be true. And we live in a world that is constantly giving us messages consciously and unconsciously, that we're not good enough, we're not thin enough, we're not rich enough, we're not successful enough, and that becomes the story which we live by. Affirmations are one way to plant new, more helpful thought seeds. Saying them over and over creates new neural pathways which strengthen over time, and then we start to focus and believe these, instead of the old thoughts that no longer serve us,' she says.

She understood my need for success—and even my need to often overcompensate because of my illness—and urged me to look beyond it. 'You were seeking a definition that you had in your head of success—that I would reach a particular point, and then I'll know that I'm good enough. Whereas that becomes this constant feeling of emptiness within you, that nothing I do is good enough, because the more you achieve something, then that's not good enough, because you've already achieved it. And there's always this lust for more which is then fuelled in the outside environment.

'For you, just affirming to go back within is connecting with your spiritual practices as well, because what our spiritual practices say is that the answers don't lie outside, the answers lie inside, the peace doesn't lie outside, the peace lies inside. It's going to realign you with your spiritual self, which is to go within, then seek that peace within, seek that security and create that space for yourself with it.'

Once again, my journal says it all.

18 July 2016: Back home after summer break in London and Germany

What was making me feel down? Post-holiday blues, but beyond that—a nagging sense of insecurity or inadequacy *at not being successful enough, not talented enough, not clever enough, not clued in enough, not hardworking enough.* I am still haunted by the spectre of success, by the promise of talent and its rigorous pursuit. This feeling of inadequacy is heightened during conversations with high-achieving friends and mentors in the UK, whose intellect and success are enhanced by their values, especially compassion and sensitivity, that I would like to emulate. And so the easiest thing I can say to myself: *I am still not good enough.* What am I doing to make a dent in this universe? Look at XYZ and see where he/she is, as a writer, as a thought leader, as a creative artist.

Yet, when I reflect on it, as Sandhini said, creative pursuits are about looking at your own yoga mat, and not being distracted by the perceived harmony in someone else's mat. I need to find the balance of movement and stillness, the acceptance of both alignment and friction, of bricks and voids, in myself.

. . . Purpose and meaning. Even though I feel I've shouted myself hoarse on this subject, I still find myself going around in circles on it. Being able to make a dent in the universe—however tiny—is part of my DNA.

3. Mid-2013, Mumbai

My close friend and interior architect Radhika Desai and I are wandering the streets of Mumbai, exploring furniture, lights and all the fun stuff that goes into designing and planning a home.

In between our store visits, we exchange ideas, for writing, for books, on the world. This is our third collaboration—we have previously worked on essays for a book, on a column in the Mint, and now my new home.

Our conversations shepherd me closer towards my latent creative spirit. I begin to realize that when the churning in my head makes its way on the screen, when fragments of notes come together into a finished work, when I can press the 'send' button and share it, I am fulfilled. Writing is a primeval life-force that sustains me. Fractured as my mind has been on so many occasions, my collaborations with Radhika narrate a tale of redemption: my mind is whole, especially when channelled into creativity.

'I have never felt that you have been in any way compromised in your working situation because of your bipolarity. In all three phases, there was a synergy. You were always excited and charged in a very positive and very normal way, on every interaction we had. If sometimes you were just not 100 per cent after a point, that happens to me too. Maybe we're all on a spectrum! I certainly don't put it beyond myself that I sometimes have highs and lows or that I go through creative moments or down moments. And when you are working with somebody who's on the same wavelength, you don't think of it as an aberration. I have not seen that with you. Honestly, you've spoken about it, but I have not seen it.'

She dissects my creative approach. 'I think you thrive when there is an unknown factor, and you have to work in a direction where the outcome of a creative endeavour is not known. I think it gives you a lot of energy and it keeps you engaged in a clear and unhindered way. You also like to make connections between areas that are not necessarily the usual things that people will think of. So whether it is business and design or even in your home and the way you thought about it. You think like a creative person, you don't think like a management person. I mean, your first mind is your creative mind. Your second mind is your management mind.' So great to hear this!

For Radhika, 'writing is the medium for you to clarify your thinking, to pour out your generative self, it's the deeper aspect of a creative self. And in writing, you are able to channel it fully. From the germ to the tip of the tree, it comes out in your writing. But the alignment of the emotion, the passion and the intellect have to remain, all through. The minute it veers into the direction of either passionlessness, or the opposite, which is more likely, which is when passion and intellect get subsumed, the writing ends up being nothing. It implodes. So, as in the best poetry and the best prose, the tighter it is, the more refined is the thinking behind the final form. You *have* to aim for that. And then it takes on its own energy and form, and it goes beyond you, and it appeals universally.'

My psychiatrist in London, Dr Shanahan, concurs. 'Initially, you were far more inclined to link being slightly high with creativity. And although the truth can run hand in hand, sometimes the high can push the creativity to a place where it's not productive. And I think you've learned to match your feelings and your creativity in a way that gives you much better productivity. And that's been a big change in you.'

The discussion with Atmapadma set me off on a journey to seek my own path, independent of the family business. The affirmations from Tara led me to look within and be kinder to myself. And the long-standing friendship and collaboration with Radhika pointed me towards an avenue of fertile self-expression.

All these exchanges were vital in getting me to have deep conversations with myself; my self-therapy on the subjects of purpose, identity and meaning. And I'm happy to say, I progressed over the years, as I recorded in my journal.

The sale of the family business in August 2012 forced me to examine my capabilities, as I wrote:

December 2012

One of the biggest internal struggles for me has been to deal with the perception—particularly amongst businesspeople—that journalism is "inferior" to running a business, and that if I'm not running a business, I'm a failure or not as successful as I could be. Their logic is understandable—a huge balance sheet is, of course, a great asset in life. It is natural for me to wonder what I'm doing every time I interview a CEO. And traces of my entrepreneurial instinct drive me to continually scan the horizon for new business opportunities.

If I have to be true to myself, I must acknowledge my strengths and weaknesses. I prefer managing ideas over people, time and money; solitude is a necessity for me, deadlines and too much multitasking is damaging. I must believe in myself and work towards my strengths: I think I have the ability to come up with some really interesting insights and narratives—fiction and non-fiction—and I need to work much harder in honing my craft, my writing skills, and my knowledge to get myself to a place where I can aspire to be a great writer and make a meaningful contribution to our society's understanding of itself.

Khozem was absolutely right: writing is healing, and writing about something challenging has given me intellectual confidence. At this point in time, I have the luxury of picking projects, I must have the courage to pursue an alternative path and work towards excelling in it.

At the risk of being cliché, I need to remind myself of my favourite sayings, also from J.B. Petit days:

To thine own self be true, and it must then follow as the night unto the day, that thou canst not then be false to any man (from Shakespeare's Hamlet).

Dare to be different
Dare to stand alone
Dare to have a purpose true
Dare to make it known. (Anon).

By May 2013, a few months after coming back from Bihar and after my mess-ups at the *Mint*, I began to be more accepting of my limitations and become more compassionate with myself, as I wrote in my journal:

14 May 2013

I still need to craft a narrative/image of myself, one that is satisfying, fulfilling and achievable. Need to ask myself: What is success? What is purpose? What is meaning? What is happiness? Must it be about money, fame, position, power, prestige? Should one set goals for one's career? Am I getting troubled with the fact that my peers are "achieving more" than me at my age? Or should one just focus on the task at home and doing it well: the craftsmanship approach?

. . . Accept: my career has had a triple whammy in the last seven to eight years (change of industries and roles [from business to journalism], marriage and relocation [to London and back] and motherhood, and bipolar disorder). So it's important to just take it step-by-step and try and resurrect it, rather than trying to be a super-achiever and failing.

My goal is to remain grounded, happy and stable for the next five years. That's a big achievement for me. Just as I don't like being "down", I should be wary of going too "up".

Towards the end of that year, I documented all the major events of the year in my annual year-end 'list'. It highlights my willingness to adopt a slower pace of professional growth.

12 November 2013

I think for the first time, I'm beginning to appreciate the value of simplicity and spontaneity, alongside power and purpose. If I go through the list above, what really stands out for me is how much time I've spent with the boys this year, and how much I've enjoyed it—I wouldn't want to change that. I'm beginning to realize that I don't need to curtail my ambition, I just need to figure out how to pace it better, and make sure that I can maintain a balance at all times. Being part of the rat race and making it by a certain age in life doesn't work for me—I just need to make sure I'm on the right path towards fulfilling my goals, whether that happens at fifty or sixty.

For example, I'm gaining more confidence in my ability to generate original ideas. I now need to find ways to develop them and to find the right platforms and relationships through which I can express them: I need to make this a priority for 2014.

Three years later, I was clearly happier with the direction of my new 'portfolio' life, as I reflected on my year-end 'list' for 2016.

23 November 2016

> It's apparent that I'm doing a number of things: interviewing and writing, speaking and presenting, researching books, co-hosting a book club, fundraising, piano, travel and, of course, kids and family. *This is my life, and I love it.*

Finally, an entry in the early part of 2018 highlights how much I had evolved in seeing myself as a writer. I came back delighted from the Jaipur Literature Festival (JLF), the second time I had attended it.

Monday, 29 January 2018

> Went to JLF, and this time I really felt engaged:
>
> *As audience:* I concentrated on the one-on-one conversations rather than the panels, and it was just amazing to see writers like Tom Stoppard, Rupi Kaur (and her fan following), Michael Rezendes (*Boston Globe/Spotlight*) and Julia Donaldson on stage. All have such distinct personalities that result in such distinct voices and thus such distinct positioning in their audience's heads—this point really came home to me this year.
>
> *As a tribe member:* just great to run into so many fellow writers, columnists and journalists during the festival and at its parties, especially the stunning Penguin party.

As a writer: fantastic conversations with Namita Gokhale (so excited about the writing retreat), publishers, retailers and others . . . this is the single most important weekend of the year from a work point of view for me. It's great that it's in Jan and sets the agenda for the rest of the year in terms of priorities. Once again, happy, thankful and grateful, no matter how things turn out.

And this is how I made the leap from dejection on ejection from the family business 'ladder' to delivering a talk on the benefits of a 'jungle-gym career'. Self-doubt continues to stab me from time to time, but I am more able to rise above it when it attacks.

Seema Bhangar, a close schoolfriend with whom I had exchanged many notes on the subject, applauds my shift. 'This has been a very significant period of five years for you professionally, and for forging your current professional identity. You have made a real pivot, and wrestled these demons of idealism, identity, ambition. It's not easy—and especially challenging with the bipolar overlay. Life is so for all of us, but for you in particular it's been a hero's journey. These are, in part, universal themes of midlife and the life of a so-called "high achieving" working mother. Good on you for diving into the bear pit.'

Self-therapy is a practice I try and employ when I am feeling low too. For example, I try and mentally dissociate myself from the emotions of depression (unhappiness, despair, a sense of bleakness or failure) and tell myself, quite confidently: this is not who I am. If mania preys on my vulnerabilities, my internal sense of self serves as 'armour' against depression. I remind myself of my mental image of myself as someone optimistic, curious and friendly, not someone held hostage to my melancholy feelings.

I conjure the image of depression as an 'external' entity, as writer Andrew Solomon, the author of *The Noonday Demon: An Atlas of Depression*, suggests. He likens depression to a 'huge vine that had attached itself to a confident oak tree and had nearly smothered it. It was hard to say where the tree left off and the vine began . . . my depression had grown on me as that vine had completely conquered the oak; it had been a sucking thing that had wrapped itself around me, ugly and more alive than I. It had a life of its own that bit by bit asphyxiated all of life out of me.'[2]

My depression has been milder and a different metaphor comes to mind. I am now accustomed to greeting depression as one might greet a temporary, unwelcome neighbour—with grudging familiarity and tolerance, until they leave.

My self-therapy also includes my own 'self-fulfilling happiness prophecy'. This was developed at business school. Just before I fell asleep, I would make myself think of any single event I enjoyed during the day. It could be something as trivial as a yoga class, a creative writing lesson, a bike ride on the river or coffee with friends.

This resulted in a virtuous cycle: I kept looking out for things to do during the day that I would reflect on before I went to sleep, with the consequence that I was feeling happy during the day too, doing all the things I enjoy doing. I remember going to meet my counsellor at business school and sharing this little 'self-fulfilling happiness prophecy' with her and she said: 'it's as simple as that?' I said: 'Yes.' Of course, I had to go to class and do my coursework, but I would make time for simple daily joys.

● ● ●

Namrata Nayyar-Kamdar is another example of the power of self-therapy. An old friend, she is a London-based entrepreneur and the founder of Plenaire, a pioneering skincare and beauty brand. A seasoned corporate professional, she was diagnosed with depressive illness and work-related stress after the birth of her second child. The situation deteriorated to such an extent that she couldn't work, concentrate, focus or take even a minor decision, she says. Constant rumination and regrets about the past, and irritability and anger about minor issues plagued her, as did early morning waking, intrusive thoughts and inability to go back to sleep.

Eventually, she left her employer and began a period of intensive therapy at the Priory, one of London's leading mental health institutions, for nearly a year. After coming out of therapy, she started her company, Plenaire (which stands for 'in the open' in French).

Her specific circumstances differ, yet her learnings parallel mine. 'It is all about yourself. This is what I learnt from my own experiences, that when something bad happens to you—whether your spouse falls ill, or in my case, whatever happened at work, or you lose a job, you get into some financial difficulty—the way that you cope is by claiming a victim narrative. "Why me? Why is this happening to me?" This is all being done to me as though I'm a passive passenger and my circumstances control me. And what I learnt when I went into therapy is to change my way of thinking. By creating a positive construct. I learnt that everything is a choice. You can choose to be victimized by it, or you can choose to rise from the ashes. You can treat anything as a problem, or you can treat it as a set of circumstances that is going to help one grow, to get you to a better place.'

Just like it was for me, her journey was agonizing, but ultimately, led to a meaningful destination. 'I had this idea from my parents, or from the people in my circle who know me, of what success looks like. And I had to work really hard on myself to let go of what people think or other people's ideas of success. And to realize that happiness, and therefore success, is a choice and could look like something else. Before my health crises, I never thought I was good enough. I felt ashamed but also powerless to change my own circumstances. I felt out of control and I accepted it when I was told that I wasn't good at something or took it extremely personally when I was criticized, getting angry, bitter or defensive,' she admits.

Now, she acknowledges the value of other people's opinions but doesn't let them affect her actions or feelings about herself. She also values her pivot, from corporate professional to entrepreneur. 'I really strongly believe that transition and change are necessary conditions to grow. If I hadn't evolved at that stage, if I hadn't changed, I would have stayed unhappy. I had to change. I was ready to change. I had actually, in some ways, outgrown my circumstances at the time, and my employer. I realized that I needed greater autonomy, freedom to create, and that continuing to do what I was doing was not going to make me happy. Second, I was able to get back my own self-worth, recognizing that I wasn't being valued correctly, which was a sign to build my own equity. I had built up equity about who I was from my family, from my employer, but now I wanted to build my own. Namrata Kamdar, "What is she good at? What does she stand for? What is she going to be known for?"

'It was a turning point, a leadership journey, but one that felt like a huge relief, almost being released from a cage. Following the departure from what had been a long period of depressive illness, via self-therapy, it was as if a light had been switched on in a different part of my brain. My amygdala wasn't paralysed with anxiety. I wasn't constantly trying to defend my actions. I actually experienced things differently, food tasted better, colours looked brighter. I started to experience feeling emotions more intensely and beauty more viscerally; it was as if I had been viewing the world through smudgy glass, which had finally been replaced by a vortex of sparkling light. That's what positive thinking, mindfulness and deep relaxation techniques did for me,' she says.

Her experiences with mental health and therapy directly informed the genesis of Plenaire. 'Now my identity is quite wrapped up in what I learnt through this experience. Working on Plenaire has given me a lot of licence to explore these issues with a younger set of people who are unsure, who are also suffering. At the core of the proposition that we've developed in our brand is mental health and well-being, not just because I went through that situation, but because when we went and we did the research with young people, a lot of the conversations in beauty, funnily enough, came back to comparisons. Not thin enough, not rich enough, not blonde enough.'

The techniques that she learnt about strengthening her mental health (staying grounded in nature, compassion, gratitude, mindfulness) built her awareness about conquering shame and altering one's narrative of oneself. 'How you were raised, your childhood, your own tendencies to compare yourself, your feelings of worry or anxiety that somebody might be judging you, these are all normal human feelings. We have them all the time, and to be able to talk about them openly is extremely important,' she says, concluding with her favourite mantra, 'If you are depressed you are living in the past. If you are anxious you are living in the future. If you are at peace you are living in the present.'

● ● ●

This chapter's poem is a piece on spending time with oneself. I wrote it a few years ago, during a pause in a personal war that had besieged me for over a decade at the time. I wanted to chronicle the different aspects of solitude I had experienced over the years since my condition is internal rather than external. Solitude is often interpreted negatively, but for me it is very layered. This piece was at the back of my mind for a long time, and it was satisfying to have it come together, even though it looks so simple at first glance.

Solitude

Solitude is disguise
The empty space between
Two people on a six-foot bed

Solitude is escape
A personal TV in a hotel room
In a midlands factory town

Solitary is privacy
Moments of aimless anonymity
In airport cafés and lounges

Solitude is retreat
The front passenger seat
A carful of preschoolers and nannies at the back

Solitude is sensory overload
Inhabiting a manic reality
Tortured and ecstatic

Solitude is silence
A struggle for words
And thoughts

Solitude is sanctuary
A personal workspace
With no blind spots

Solitude is peace
When an inner war
Has been won

Solitude is joy
In the knowledge
That happiness multiplies
But never through acquisition

Solitude is faith
A hope held close
And a prayer for lasting peace

The meeting last year with Radhanath Maharaj at the ISKCON temple, which Chacha took me to, was a pivotal conversation. He gave me practical tools to live with my disorder and also to cement my faith. Don't feel guilty about being bipolar, take your medicines, keep life simple, have gratitude, and do mala, puja and pray, he said.

6 February 2017
(extract from journal)

9

The Life-Changing Tributaries of Spiritual Therapy

June 2017, London

It is well past dawn when I have a soul orgasm. I wake up around 6 a.m., much earlier than normal, full of devotional energy, needing a walk. I put on my headset, turn on the 'spiritual playlist' on my phone, wear my sports shoes and walk across to Primrose Hill, one of London's most popular parks. This is my family's annual summer holiday and I have drifted into hypomania.

I climb the hill and take in the view of the famous London Zoo, the city's iconic skyline and the park's rich greenery. A quote by the English poet William Blake, inscribed in stone at the summit of the hill, makes me pause. 'I have conversed with the spiritual sun. I saw him on Primrose Hill.' So, I am not the only one to have a metaphysical encounter!

Bhajans play on as I descend the hill. I am struck by ideas for affirmations on one's dharma and record these phrases on my phone, with unconstrained passion and emotion. The few walkers and joggers in the park would have no doubt assumed that I was talking to myself.

On the way back home, there is a light drizzle. One of my favourite bhajans, 'Guru Brahma Guru Vishnu' comes on. And suddenly I feel as if my soul has shattered into millions of pieces of sweetness and pleasure as I surrender to a higher power. I feel as if I am touched by the Almighty himself. 'I am blessed, I am blessed, I am blessed,' I yell as loudly as I can, arms outstretched, reaching for the sky. It doesn't matter if a man cleaning the front porch of the house I had just walked past looks strangely at me. I'm having a soul orgasm.

Of course, even though I think I've been touched by divinity, I know it is not possible to go home and greet the children in such an excitable state. I do a few high-knees and other boot camp-style exercises on the pavement until I'm out of breath and have calmed down. I type furiously into my phone until the bullet points exhaust themselves. By now, I have become a little better—but possibly not very much better—at channelling and attempting to conceal my energies when I am hypomanic.

My spiritual journey has been an organic quest, with many tributaries seeming to merge into one over the years, rather than following a single guru or teacher. As the above anecdote, and my experience at the yoga ashram in Bihar, illustrate, this quest has tipped me over the edge on occasion, but on the whole, it has been a vital element of my stability.

The themes and topics I have learnt are profound, and include:

o   discovering faith
o   developing an attitude of gratitude
o   meditating through music and chanting
o   cultivating mindfulness and awareness of one's emotions
o   appreciating the distinction between mind and intellect
o   absorbing the almost levitational power of detachment

o   letting go of the downward gravitational forces of
    attachment
o   embracing struggle as positive thinking
o   distilling the rich texture of dharma, and
o   understanding the nature of the true self

Individually, these spiritual tributaries are powerful.
Collectively, they constitute life-changing therapy.

So let me take you through them and describe how I try
to navigate the inherent paradox in this most compelling
of therapies.

● ● ●

Discovering Faith

My mother is an atheist, but that did not stop her from
installing a puja ghar in our bedroom, where I spent many
hours bathing and dressing a statue of Lord Krishna as a
child. Luiza Fernandes, our devout Catholic nanny, taught us
Christian prayers, sometimes taking us to church, and created
a manger every Christmas in her personal shrine to Jesus
and Mother Mary. Close friendships with Muslim, Parsi and
Jewish friends exposed Radhika and I to the beauty of their
faiths. Our childhood was thus as secular as it could be. Yet,
though I might have been curious about faith as a child, it was
not a priority as an adolescent and young adult—certainly
much less interesting than going dancing with friends.

But my outlook shifted when I first started doing
pregnancy yoga in my early thirties in 2008 at Homevilla
Yoga, an Iyengar yoga centre in Mumbai run by the energetic
Ina Dani. Here is a note I wrote to Inaben a few years later
in 2014, on the death of her guru B.K.S. Iyengar, about my
experience at her centre.

Balancing on Faith: A Tribute to Guruji B.K.S. Iyengar and Inaben Dani

Faith can be discovered in the most unexpected places. I experienced it in an undignified position: head down, legs sticking up, body resting against an armless chair and a huge baby bump blocking my view. I felt it again when I held on to two ropes suspended from the ceiling, legs crossed and strapped up against the wall, looking as agile as a pregnant Spiderman.

This is maternity yoga at the Iyengar yoga centre run by the venerable Inaben Dani. To first-time observers, it is always a revelation. A dozen pregnant women contort themselves into positions that are usually assumed to be well beyond their capabilities. There is the occasional murmur, but otherwise everyone follows a quiet personal routine, mentally calibrating her turn at each station, adjusting pillows, bricks and ropes to suit her needs, monitored by Inaben and her assistants.

Faith is a multicoloured bird. At the Iyengar centre, I discovered a particular expression of it, *a blend of grace, wisdom and purity and an understanding of what it means to serve*.

I agreed to lower myself into a modified headstand because I trusted Inaben's wisdom and her belief in her guru, the late B.K.S. Iyengar. I was there twice or thrice a week, for several months, even during the second pregnancy. Twenty asanas, and ninety-minute sessions, watching leafy trees, dark skies, or sunlit windows. It was a time dedicated to silence, to the purity of perfection, to finding stillness amongst movement.

For once, my body was not asked to speed up, or to do more repetitions or more challenging postures. It just wanted me to be mindful and perform each asana with focus, attention and care.

> Pregnancy is an inward-looking phase in a woman's life, where we are constantly reminded to take care of ourselves, our bodies, our minds, our diet, our sleep, our moods, our hormones, our cravings. But at Inaben's centre, I learnt what it means to serve a new life; I assimilated the Hindu expression that to serve babies is to serve God.
>
> Somewhere during those many months I came to realize that I wasn't just doing the yoga because it was therapeutic, because I felt calm or peaceful, or lighter or even because (as I liked to say) it "helped me get more comfortable with my bump". I was doing this because somewhere inside there was a new life, a tiny, crinkled, wriggly little creature with a beating heart, whose purity I was celebrating.
>
> My deliveries were straightforward and my children, aged six and three, are healthy and vocal. It is the most joyous blessing a parent can seek. Thank you, Guruji and Inaben, for sharing your divinity, wisdom and inner light.

As Rabindranath Tagore said, 'faith is the bird that feels the light when the dawn is still dark'. This bird was beginning to reveal itself to me.

Attitude of Gratitude

My budding interest in faith was fortified by one of the biggest influences in my spiritual evolution—Ajay Chacha, who has studied Hindu scriptures for decades with his teachers. We have spoken on the subject on many occasions, and some incidents are particularly memorable, starting with this journal entry, which I wrote after coming back from the yoga ashram in Bihar:

3 May 2013

It's been a difficult two months—I think I've been the closest I've been to depression, mostly because I didn't know what to do with myself and my non-existent career.

Some conclusions I've reached: Attitude of gratitude: I'm lucky. I have what 99 per cent of people (especially women) do not have in this world: family, great kids, supportive extended family, comfortable home, no financial troubles, no need to work. Better to concentrate on those rather than worry about what the other 1 per cent might have that I don't.

'Attitude of gratitude' has really helped me get on the first few rungs of the self-constructed ladder that I believe takes me out of my black hole. On its own, the motto might seem insufficient to pull someone back from the brink of despair. But its power lies in its ability to make the mind receptive to more positive messaging to come. I went to meet Ajay Chacha around the time I wrote this journal entry and discussed the notion of gratitude with him. He affirmed that gratitude is an essential aspect of all religions across the world; it appeals to our higher selves. It is an attitude—and it does not depend on being in the top 1 per cent or 10 per cent or any statistic. If we just stop to look around us, all of us have so much more to be grateful for than we imagine.

A direct corollary of 'attitude of gratitude' is giving and sharing, and I have tried to make my giving more strategic and structured by advising non-profits or grant-giving. Actually, I have come to realize that giving means getting back as I gain emotional and intellectual fulfilment and validation. The purpose of life is a life of purpose, or so the saying goes. Seed-funding a campaign to provide role models to adolescents, sponsoring therapy for daughters of sex workers, fundraising for a technology-for-health non-profit have all given me purpose. My philanthropic efforts might be small monetarily but they have made a difference, and I have met some incredible individuals along the way.

● ● ●

Meditation through Music and Chanting

February 2017, Mumbai

My friend Saumya and I decide to attend the Kala Ghoda Festival on a whim, to listen to an artist named Sonam Kalra & the Sufi Gospel Project, never having heard her music and attracted by the name of the band. It is my most serendipitous spiritual encounter. The multifaith, contemporary, soulful quality of her work is hugely evocative. So much so that the first time I hear her rendition of 'Amazing Grace' a few days later, sitting at the back of the car on my way home from an event, silent tears escape me. I had always liked the hymn, and finally, I find a version that I love.

> *Through many dangers, toils and snares,*
> *We have already come.*
> *T'was grace that brought us safe thus far,*
> *And grace will lead us home.*

These lyrics—and the hymn in general—are now a personal talisman that I turn to as often as possible. I am now an official Sonam Kalra groupie, having downloaded her music on my phone, watched her videos, dragged Amit to attend her concerts in small arts venues in Mumbai and even emailed her, connecting through a common friend. Formal meditation is not encouraged for me by my doctors, but I like to think of my spiritual playlist, of which Sonam's work is a major element, as my meditation, through music. Pandit Jasraj, to whom I was introduced by Ajay Chacha, is also a favourite. And I never imagined that 'Humko Man Ki Shakti', a bhajan we were forced to learn growing up, could be such a lifeline in times of distress, but it is.

Selections from my seven-hour-long spiritual playlist (always open to suggestions to expand this!):

'Vandana' by Pandit Jasraj
'Om Namo Bhagwate Vasudevaya' by Pandit Jasraj
'Rani Tero Chirjeeyo Gopal' by Pandit Jasraj
'Govind Damodar Madhaveti' by Pandit Jasraj
'Gopal Niranjan' by Pandit Jasraj
'Achyutam Keshavam'—three versions, by Suresh Wadkar, Anup Jalota and Vikram Hazra
Vaishnava Jana To'—two versions, by Lata Mangeshkar and Shivali
'Gayatri Mantra' by Shankar Mahadevan
'Hanuman Chalisa' by Pankaj Udhas
'Gurur Brahma Gurur Vishnu' by Jagjit Singh
'Om Jai Jagdish Hare' by Shankar Mahadevan
'Maa Tujhe Salaam' by A.R. Rahman
'O Paalanhaare' by A.R. Rahman, Lata Mangeshkar and Udit Narayan
'Shree Krishna Chaitanya' by Sachin Limaye

'Tvameva Mata' by Rosa Ena Campos
'Raghupati Raghav Raja Ram'—instrumental and vocal
'Man Manam' by Sonam Kalra & the Sufi Gospel Project
'The Amazing Grace Prayer' by Sonam Kalra & the Sufi Gospel Project
'The Confluence' by Sonam Kalra & the Sufi Gospel Project
'In the Garden' by Sonam Kalra & the Sufi Gospel Project
'Hallelujah I Just Love Him So' by Sonam Kalra & the Sufi Gospel Project
'Abide with Me' by Sonam Kalra & the Sufi Gospel Project
'Alfat' by Sonam Kalra & the Sufi Gospel Project
'Humko Mann Ki Shakti Dena' by A.R. Rahman

Chanting is equally vital. On one occasion, when I was having trouble sleeping, I shared my troubles with Ajay Chacha, telling him that I chant at night to try and fall asleep. 'What do you chant,' he asked. I mumbled something about 'Gobind bolo, Gopal bolo', a line from a popular bhajan.

He picked up a book on mantras and pointed to a particular page:

Hare Ram Hare Ram
Ram Ram Hare Hare
Hare Krishna Hare Krishna
Krishna Krishna Hare Hare

Perhaps the most famous, and simplest, of Hindu mantras, but he explained it to me as gently as one would to a child. His patience was reassuring. I invoke the mantra at night when I need help sleeping, even if it is not (yet) a part of my daily spiritual practice.

● ● ●

Cultivating Mindfulness and Emotional Awareness, and Learning the Distinction Between Body, Mind and Intellect

February 2017

Back from visiting one of my medical practitioners, I am distraught. My writing on mental health has just been dismissed by them, and I go to Amit, telling him that I want to switch practitioners. He reacts defensively, reiterating how dependent he is on our practitioner for medical support during my mood swings. I lock myself in the bathroom, sob for a few minutes, pull myself together and then come out and plant myself on the living room sofa.

'Amartya's birthday is coming up. Let's not fight until then,' Amit says.

'We're not fighting even now,' I reply.

Later, I write in my journal:

> Disastrous session with XYZ on writing and its aftermath, bust up with Amit, yet amicable recovery (very proud of myself). Follow-up conversations, still unresolved.

Mindfulness is part of our zeitgeist. 'Observe the fluctuations of the mind, do not become them' is a popular quote, and one of my guiding mantras. Getting there, however, is an altogether different matter.

The youthful and articulate Swami Swatmananda Saraswati of the Chinmaya Mission and one of Ajay Chacha's spiritual teachers, elaborates on this idea. 'Awareness of an emotion requires a very high level of objectivity because generally, we tend to associate with the emotion, that's why we feel the impact of that emotion. And as they say in psychology, "if you don't feel it, you can't heal it". So one should not escape emotions, one should first use coping mechanisms to quieten the mind—that is important.

'When there is a high level of objectivity, one is able to say that this emotion is rising in my mind, but I am not the mind, I am not the emotion. Then one can stand apart from the emotion. In spiritual terminology we call this as saakshi or being a witness. It is a very advanced practice. If one is able to do that, then we are able to see how mind fuels the emotion and understand the nature of the attachment that is causing the emotion and see the reaction of the mind. One can then control the impulsive reaction that the emotion would've caused if one were not a witness. It is not easy to do. To observe one's emotions is the final step in spiritual life. One needs to build up towards that through various other practices, through identifying various attachments, trying to eliminate them. That makes the mind stronger,' he says.

I would say I am much more aware of my emotions than earlier, but I cannot always stand apart from them, on a daily basis. At best, I can 'attend' to them—give them space for expression, without being consumed by them. For example, if I feel a tinge of anger or frustration, or even when I might be bordering on euphoria, I share my feelings with my friends and family. It helps me to exhale the emotion, just as one might exhale unwanted breath.

As I wrote in my journal a few years ago:

I'm beginning to learn to think of misplaced manic thoughts as scavengers, that will feed off negative emotions such as fear, insecurity, ego, dissatisfaction, unhappiness, discontent, cravings, hatred, being needy. And I think of the positive emotions: love and affection, security, self-confidence, contentment, peace, happiness, job satisfaction, positive energy, fearlessness—as the emotional and mental "armour" that can prevent the scavengers from raiding. In other words, if there's a chink in the armour, then the scavengers can come scurrying around and will wait for an opportunity to strike. This applies to everyone of course, but perhaps being bipolar, I feel more vulnerable than most.

The concept of body, mind and intellect (BMI) provides an illuminating framework to keep the scavenging thoughts at bay and to be more mindful and aware of one's emotions. I was introduced to it by a Vedanta teacher, whose classes I attended every Saturday morning in our building clubhouse for a year in 2017.

'The body is your most external aspect. It is merely a vehicle to move your personality from one experience to another experience. The inner personality is what is interesting, and it is made up of thoughts, which are categorizable into two types. Indiscriminate, irrational, impulsive thoughts, which are classifiable as our wants and wishes, which we call our desires, impulses, emotions or feelings. These are categorized as the mind.

'Then there is the discriminate thought, our ability to reason, to be logical, rational, mature, stable. This is thinking, reasoning, analysis, judgement—these are classified as intellect. So, the human being is driven into activity of the body by either the mind, or the intellect, or a combination of both,' explains my teacher, who prefers to remain anonymous.

Intellect does not preclude humour. In fact, humour is a sign of intellect, he told us. 'You have to be light-hearted to cultivate humour within yourself, you have to have the mental space to do it. If you're constantly burdened by desires and agitated by all the various unfulfilled desires that you are needlessly generating and harbouring, there is no time to be humorous. If you're too involved in the world, if you're too attached, you won't have time to be humorous because everything is personalized. When you have an intellect, life becomes impersonal.'

A developed intellect uplifts one during low periods. 'The intellect is a shock absorber to depression,' he says. 'Depression happens when the mind cannot handle change, when there have been cumulative disappointments arising from unfulfilled desires. So, depression is a clear signal of the intellect not absorbing the shock of disappointments. If the intellect is developed, then you will not entertain so many desires to be disappointed, you will have a right assessment of the world. You can say, "it is what it is, I have to work my way around it, it is not going to work its way around me",' he underlines.

The benefits of understanding the dichotomy of mind and intellect are far-reaching. 'Intellect will give immunity against agitation,' he professes. 'Agitations are the signal of an uncontrolled mind, full of unfulfilled desires. So as the intellect grows stronger, the mind comes more within its control. And since the desires and demands of the mind are more within its control, there is less agitation.'

This dichotomy is vital in a manic phase. I am learning to draw on rationality when my emotions seem beyond my reach. To learn to forgive, where there is anger. To draw on reason, where there is aggression. To remain grounded, where there is cause for excitement. In other words, to make myself understand that however natural these emotions might seem, they are only expressions of inner conflict, of unfulfilled desires of the mind; they do not represent reality. The emotional fault line that has triggered them must be resolved in a logical way.

And I am learning to do all of the above without letting everyone know what's going on. This is tremendously challenging. To be able to witness and reason with your emotions whilst you are at war with yourself requires self-awareness, self-control, self-restraint—and time. It can take anything from a few days to a few weeks.

It helps, in this situation, to draw on a related Vedanta nugget. 'Within you is a friend and an enemy. Every human being has a choice of action, the choice to identify with your intellect, rather than your impulses of the mind. Make the right choice, you are the friend of yourself, you make the wrong choice, you're the enemy of yourself,' says my teacher.

● ● ●

Absorbing the Almost Levitational Power of Detachment and Letting Go of the Downward Gravitational Forces of Attachment

Another pillar of spiritual therapy—across all tributaries of Hindu philosophy—is the notion of attachment and detachment. 'Attachment is defined as a self-inflected mental bondage to your environment, your mind is entangled and possessive about objects and beings in your environment. And this directly results in misery and unhappiness. Detachment is the lack of clinginess, the mental renunciation of the object. Not the physical renunciation of the object, you are still very much in the environment, very much interacting with the object or being, but you don't have any bondage to it. You are liberated, you're free,' says my Vedanta teacher.

This philosophy has brought clarity and lightness to many relationships, with friends, family, with myself, and my moods. One particular relationship with an older family friend comes to mind. She disappointed me for years, as a friend, as an elder, both emotionally and financially, in her inability, or unwillingness, to reciprocate friendship and affection. This tangible absence in my life was a trigger, on some occasions, sparking anger. But over time, I've learnt to detach. I realized that I was the only one getting upset in the relationship, the only one suffering repeated moods swings. And over time, I have come to absorb that detachment doesn't mean indifference. I still hold affection towards her, just without concurrent expectations. It's been quite a journey getting to this place. My Vedanta lessons have reinforced this insight of learning to levitate with detachment.

● ● ●

Embracing Struggle as Positive Thinking

One of Swami Swatmananda's most memorable discourses was when he quoted the great Hindu monk, thinker and reformer, Swami Vivekananda, who said: 'Struggle, struggle, was my motto for the last ten years. Struggle, still say I. When it was all dark, I used to say, struggle; when light is breaking in, I still say, struggle. Be not afraid, my children.'

I understood what Swami Vivekananda meant when he referred to his decade-long struggle. He sacrificed so much to travel across India as a monk, living for years in poverty before securing a place on the world stage. But why would he want to continue to struggle when the 'light is breaking in'?

Swamiji answers my question. 'The mind sees hope, sees light coming in. The effort is to lift the mind to the state of light and to live there. But the mind has tendencies, it can go back to darkness or despair. If a human being stops struggling, chances are the human being will become completely complacent because if I'm not putting in an effort to rise, the mind doesn't know, it stagnates, it will fall down, it will drop. I should always ask myself, "what is it that I'm struggling out of right now?" Otherwise, we get into a comfort zone that one should avoid.'

This is a vital lesson. Bipolarity is not going away. I have to live with it for the rest of my life.

Medicines are supportive at best; they are not a cure. And all aspects of it are a struggle. Usually I submit to mania, but on some occasions, I have fought this intruder, and it has been a struggle, me versus me, mind versus intellect.

Post-mania recovery is always a struggle—facing up to the crash-landing of my delusions of grandeur and tackling a sense of disappointment, embarrassment and maybe even culpability. I struggle to reconstruct my everyday life, relying on the healing rituals of children's play dates and gym sessions. Even everyday life, with its amplified fluctuations, can be a struggle. Weight loss is a permanent struggle of my adult life.

Rather than looking at struggle as an antagonist, it is more fruitful for me to look at my struggle, and my efforts to manage my mood swings, as something positive—as a vehicle for self-growth—not a burden I must endure. Only then will I succeed in maintaining stability and harmony.

For motivation, when I am low, I turn to another Gita shloka:

> *Perform your prescribed actions,*
>> *For action is certainly better*
>> *Than inaction.*

And even the subsistence
            Of one's body cannot be
            Accomplished without action[1]

Chapter 3, Verse 8

I ask Swami Swatmananda Saraswati for an explanation. 'When one goes into that state of despair and hopelessness, then one doesn't feel like doing anything, so action is necessary. Even your bodily functions and the maintenance of body will not happen if you become completely inactive, so it is very important to keep oneself creatively occupied and dynamic even in daily life, for example with exercise, and also keep oneself inspired with goals. When actions are directed towards a goal, and if that goal is in tune with who you are, then that becomes the best action.'

● ● ●

Distilling the Rich Texture of Dharma

February 2018, Mumbai

Jetsunma Tenzin Palmo looks frail, but speaks with a blend of compassion, wisdom and authority that is the hallmark of the truly enlightened. A Buddhist legend, this Englishwoman from London spent twelve years meditating in a cave in the Himalayas and is today revered across the world. A large group of seekers gather for a discourse, hosted by my sister-in-law, Reshma Piramal. Jetsunma spends two days deconstructing four lines on dharma, known as the Four Dharmas of Gampopa, 1000-year-old words from a learned Buddhist monk.

Grant your blessings that my mind may follow the dharma.
Grant your blessings that my dharma practice may become the path.
Grant your blessing so that the path may clarify confusion.
Grant your blessings that confusion may arise as wisdom.[2]

I tried to keep up with her teachings as I typed my notes into my phone. What follows is a very abbreviated version on dharma; it is not possible to share everything she said.

'The most important thing is that the mind turns to the dharma, that the mind has awareness of emotions through practise and makes it into dharma. It all depends on the mind, how it is able to observe and deal skilfully with our negative emotions. Everything we do is me, me, me . . . we identify with the wrong part of our selves, it should go towards dharma . . . We are in a country where the dharma is still alive. But it is most important that we have some interest, not to waste it,' Jetsunma emphasized.

'Why are we on this path? Not just to gain wisdom, but to rouse innate compassion and help others,' she reminded us. 'Put the dharma at the centre of our life, not at the periphery. Beyond surface chatter. Dharma is the yeast in the midst of the heavy dough that is our life. It just needs a little bit of yeast to transform it from something heavy to something that is delicious, light bread, if only we're open and aware. We know when our practice is working when people say— "you're a nicer person".'

She quoted a popular saying: '"Life is a classroom for the souls". If the lessons are too easy, then you will get bored. Yet the effort should be effortless. Dharma is not an endurance test; it should be cheerful and joyful. Dharma practice should really take us somewhere, not just outer manifestation, it's about the inward change. We should have a sense of travelling, that we're moving. When things go wrong, we can watch how we spontaneously respond—as a worldly person or detached, with compassion. For example, Tibetan refugees were calm and cheerful when they arrived in India, despite the trauma they had gone through.' The Buddhist dharma practice, as I remember her saying it, is about loving kindness, compassion, rejoicing in others' joy, and impartiality and equality.

Just four lines can have so much impact. The discourse helped me grasp the nature of dharma in a nuanced way. Her metaphor of the yeast in the dough is wonderful and makes me want to be a better person.

❦ ❦ ❦

Understanding the Nature of the True Self

Being able to differentiate between one's emotions and one's self has made me question the nature of my true self. If I am not my feelings, strong as they are, then who am I?

I remembered a comment by a family friend, someone who is blunt and selective with his words. I'd apologized to him because I thought I'd offended him during one of my heated manic phases and he wrote back to me: 'I like very much your warm, positive, candid, intelligent, energetic manner, so how can there be any room for offence at all?' I liked the way he summarized my personality, and it was a step in the right direction for me to realize that there was more to me than the passion I associate so much with my personality and with my condition.

Swami Swatmananda provides further clarity. 'When we say, "Who am I?" then from the deepest spiritual knowledge point of view, the answer is that I am not this individuality at all. This individuality is like a role in a movie, just like the actor is completely different from the role that he assumes. Maybe Amitabh Bachchan plays a role of, let us say, a coolie, but he is not that at all. From that highest standpoint, our true self is what we call infinite consciousness or *satchitanand* and that is the same in everyone. It is one infinite consciousness, which is appearing in so many individualities. That is the deepest level of spiritual realization.'

● ● ●

B.K.S. Iyengar, Swami Chinmayananda Saraswati, Swami Swatmananda Saraswati, my Vedanta teacher and Jetsunma Tenzin Palmo are highly evolved spiritual masters. I'm lucky to have learnt from them, or their disciples, in person. The various modes of learning—yoga, prayer, meditation through music, live (and recorded) discourse and teachings from ancient texts—constitute a holistic path for any seeker.

Despite all this teaching, why was I psychotic in the ashram in January 2012? Why did I find myself yelling in the streets of London in June 2017? Why did I write dialogues for Krishna in a ski resort in Switzerland in March 2018?

Because my mind was still getting carried away, this time with passion for a higher power. In my manic highs, I looked to faith as a form of self-expression to try and find meaning in my life. I looked to faith to reinforce the notion that I was the centre of the universe and that I was chosen to lead a mission to do God's work. This is not spirituality, this is not religion, this is not faith, it is ego. It is the mind leading me astray.

I remind myself of a statement by my Vedanta teacher. 'Ego comes from the mind and self-respect comes from the intellect. Self-glorification is self-gratification, self-absorption is the ego functioning through the mind. Whereas self-respect arises from self-analysis and discrimination. You analyse yourself and come to understand your potential as a human being, you respect that potential, and you strive to reach it and maximize it.' In other words, I do not need to feel I'm 'chosen' to be blessed by God or to feel validated in life. This divinity is in me if I only care to reflect on it. I don't need to run to the top of Primrose Hill at 6 a.m. to find it.

My experiences represent a common pitfall, though. Dr Shanahan, my psychiatrist in London, points out the fine line between having belief and losing balance because of it. He affirms the benefits of 'believing in God, faith, religion, church, or the afterlife. Those things are terribly important because they give further meaning to your life. It becomes another branch of the therapy tree and is really valuable. But if it becomes too charismatic, and the quasi-religious behaviour turns manic, then one has to be very careful.'

Bhairavi, my friend who was with me at the yoga ashram, recalls its tremendous energies. 'Obviously, they know that what they're doing out there is very, very profound and effective. There was one night, we did a night meditation with a crystal Shiva linga. And we did a lot of chanting, and there was some massive energy. I felt it was like our energy field out there, like a vortex, almost like Harry Potter. There is definitely something about the place, it is very blessed and we got to see it.'

Atmapadma, my Bihar School of Yoga teacher, explains why ashrams can sometimes exude a little more magnetic energy than desired: 'I have seen a couple of people have full-on psychotic episodes in the ashram. Many ashrams, for whatever reason, either where they're situated geologically, or the fact that they're a particular kind of environment, have a very strong effect on the mind. When I first went to Bihar School, I had lots of vivid dreams. And then sometimes I would find myself crying, releasing a lot of sadness. I didn't understand it because I hadn't experienced anything like that before. I think some places do affect us at a deeper mental or psychological or even psychic level. It can be cathartic for many people.'

The relationship between spiritual therapy and mental health is layered, then. When misinterpreted, whether intentionally or accidentally, spirituality can be destructive to mental health. But when harnessed correctly, it is one of the most incredible avenues for self-discovery, mental stability and peace.

And when intertwined with conventional psychiatry, it can make mental health accessible to those who might need it most. The 'dawa–dua' experiments in Gujarat and Tamil Nadu are a fascinating example of this blending of traditional healing with modern medicine. The 550-year-old dargah (grave) of a Muslim saint located 100 km from Ahmedabad is 'well-known for treating the unexplained ailments related to the world of ghosts and djinns, especially mental and behavioural problems'[3] and popular amongst pilgrims seeking solace for such issues, says The Altruist, a mental health non-profit involved in the programme.

Local authorities decided to connect health professionals with traditional faith healers, 'educating them on mental health and on signs and symptoms of mental illness so that they could refer patients for medical treatment, create awareness on mental health and ensure continuity of care.' Mental health services were provided to 'those suffering from psychological problems visiting the dargah'.[4]

The programme is a tremendous success and has also spawned followers in a town called Erwadi in Tamil Nadu, where another ancient shrine has allowed modern medicine to be practised alongside traditional religious rituals. A clinic run by local mental health professionals has been established within the shrine's premises, offering comprehensive psychiatric care.

'Patients were counselled to continue their prayers alongside professional medical treatment and return for follow-up visits to improve their well-being. As a result of this initiative, over 3000 people suffering from mental illness have been diagnosed and treated. Over one-third of them have made follow-up visits, while others have been referred to a general hospital or placed in the care of a newly constructed 50-bed hospital located on the territory of the holy site. A community rehabilitation centre under the government-supported Community Mental Health Program has also been established to provide vocational training for patients, preparing them for integration into their communities,'[5] according to 'Dawa-Dua: How Medical Treatment Complements Prayer for People with Mental Illness in India', an article on the programme. Promising avenues for a scalable and accessible pathway into mental health.

● ● ●

I would like to think that these tributaries permeate daily life, making me a happier and more evolved human being, flowing as a river into a wider ocean of life. Approximately four years of equanimity is testimony that some of these jewels seem to have soaked into my intellect.

I have to admit, though, that my study of the spiritual texts has lapsed for some time now. I am enrolled in

Vedanta and Bhagavad Gita classes, but my attendance is irregular, partly because of a sense of complacency and partly because I am prioritizing other activities. My narrative of myself is as an eternal learner, so I hope I will make time for structured lessons in a tangible way. I have revived my yoga practice recently, and it centres me, helping to align mind, body and intellect. Music is equally a regular component of my spiritual therapy, enabling me to meditate on the divine. Most importantly, my faith has strengthened. I believe if Krishna thinks me strong enough to live with bipolarity, then I am capable of doing so.

One of my most private achievements in managing my thoughts and emotions is that I have been able to examine my deepest vulnerabilities—the sexual violence in my head—and distance myself from it. I chose to witness, express and release my most negative thoughts through the spoken and the written word because they allowed me to detach. The act of writing proclaims: this negative thought is in my head, but it does not own me. *I am not my trauma.*

Memories of delusions and hallucinations do not haunt me. I can summon them if I need to, but I do not make it a practice to remember them. I now know my mental sexual trauma is triggered by stress. These nightmares (which are increasingly rare) serve as a red flag for imminent turbulence, that's all. That is the power of detachment.

In a related vein, a few years ago, I compiled some notes on anger management for a friend who was struggling with it. I like to think that the note reflects my progress in understanding how to manage conflict and difficult emotions by reframing how we think of them. Here is an extract from the note:

o   Anger is a hiding place, an escape mechanism. It is *easier* to be angry than to confront WHY I'm angry. Consider this: Must I disappear into that hiding place? Do I really want to take the easy way out when it makes me unhappy? Do I have the courage to try and figure out why I'm so angry and deal with that? Maybe that will make me happier in the long run.

o   We cannot always control our emotions, but we can control our response to those emotions. Responding to angry thoughts and emotions is like putting the "remote control of our emotions" into someone else's hands. Consider this: is this YOU who is angry or someone else? If the anger is NOT ME, then why are we putting that remote control into someone else's hands? Consider this statement: I want to keep the remote control of emotion in my hands, I want to walk away from the anger, I want to take a deep breath and be calm. THAT IS ME. ANGER IS NOT ME.

o   Getting into a fit of rage may be a learned behaviour from childhood, and it may have been your defence mechanism at the time, but is it the only way to deal with a situation? It may be the intuitive response, but can you LEARN OTHER ways to deal with difficult situations? YES OF COURSE.

o   Will anger get me the outcome I want? The anger comes from a sense of fear, stress, anxiety about a certain outcome, whether that relates to the children's future or your relationship with them. So the anger comes from your love for them, its starting point is all about what you want for them and for yourself, which is good. But consider: by getting angry will you get the result you want? Will getting angry actually give you control of the outcome you seek or just a temporary illusion of control? Will getting angry make anyone happier? The answer is a straightforward no.

My most fundamental spiritual aspiration is to be dynamic and peaceful, just like when I try to perfect surya namaskars on the yoga mat. As Swami Swatmananda says, 'Being dynamic and peaceful is the combination of a healthy identity, where externally one is dynamic, but internally, one is operating out of peace, because of the work that one is doing. The work is inspiring to the person, it is the *svadharma* as we call it. If I do what I'm made for, what I truly love, then my mind internally is at peace, I have no conflict. Externally, I can set goals and I can aspire to achieve different levels in that field that I have chosen. So inner peace and external dynamism would come when I set the right goals, in my work, in my relationships, and in my personal spiritual evolution as an individual.'

Dynamism is particularly relevant in the bipolar context. My inner life is inherently dynamic. My moods will change more than most. They can impact my body and my mind. But my inner peace should be unchanging. That is my hope.

● ● ●

I wrote 'Snow' when I was hypomanic at a ski resort in Switzerland. Even though I had seen snow falling on other occasions, this fairy-tale winter wonderland took my breath away.

Snow

For some it's a slope
For others it's powder
For some it's seasonal dressing
For me it's *vairagya*

The beauty of detachment
Would the tree be so precious without its silver?
Yes, it comes and goes
But it is eternal
Nature's *Silver Linings Playbook*

But I am lost in its power
Cannot find the simple route home
As I stare at the white forest

One day I will get there
I pray to the sun
Who melts this snow
That is *vairagya*

The slope refers to the ski slope, but also the slippery slope of life. Powder refers to the snowfall, or to cocaine—how something so beautiful can also be dangerous. *Silver Linings Playbook* is a movie about being bipolar. Vairagya means detachment.

I realize I'm generally much happier following a more disciplined lifestyle—in bed by 10.30 p.m. on weekdays, no work after 8 p.m., spend time with kids at dinnertime as much as possible, 2–3 days in the office every week, interspersed with work-from-home and afternoons at home with the kids, working out with Shilpa, plans to start riding, continue with badminton and regular chanting.

19 October 2016

Just saw the *Forbes* cover—not flattering at all. Feeling so down. When did this sugar addiction kick in? I just feel awful about my body.

21 December 2018

(extracts from journals)

10

Lifestyle Therapy: Tending to the Garden of Mental Wellness

Schedule of a 'normal' day (in and out of lockdown)

7–7.30 a.m.	*Wake up and take thyroid medication*
8.30 a.m.	*Yoga or join the family for breakfast and catch up on the news (always skipping the sports section)*
10–10.30 a.m.	*At my desk, or at Soho House*
12 p.m.	*Have lunch with Agastya, followed by supplements*
12.30 p.m. onwards	*Back at my desk, writing, doing interviews, non-profit work, teaching or speaking*
4.30 p.m.	*Light evening snack at my desk*
5.30–6.30 p.m.	*A session (virtual or in the gym) with my personal trainer or a walk in the building complex or sometimes at the racecourse.*
7.30 p.m.	*Dinner with children, and Amit if he's free*
8.30 p.m.	*Take psychiatric meds*

9.00 p.m.	*Netflix or reading. Socializing with friends and family (virtual or in-person)*
10.30 p.m.	*Bedtime*
In between	*A lot of time spent on WhatsApp!*

Although it looks quite ordinary, it feels like an achievement.

Because the schedule of a manic or hypomanic day looks very different—I wake up early, maybe even as early as 4.30 a.m., and am unable to get back to bed. I am restless, pacing around the house. My heightened energy manifests itself in the gut—I make frequent trips to the bathroom and am constantly hungry, reaching for carbs and sugar. I exercise twice a day—morning yoga and long evening walks or I ask my trainer for special exercises to relax me. And unless I discipline myself or take something to help me sleep, I can stay awake until quite late at night too.

A depressed day is, of course, the opposite. I struggle to get out of bed at 8.30 a.m. and want to go straight back to bed after breakfast. I have to push myself to work, I reach for sugar after meals and am generally lethargic and sluggish, even during my workouts.

And there are days in between, anywhere on the continuum, with milder or higher peaks or lower or shallower troughs. In other words, bipolarity for me is all about managing the day, seeing if the day goes well. If it doesn't, I have to act immediately, I cannot afford to wait for a week if I find myself going off-kilter. As my friend Mary says, 'treating your mental health is like a project, something that you have to attend to every day, like a garden you have to tend to every day.'

The 'rhythm' of the day is vital in helping me adhere to a schedule. The rhythm consists of three elements, according to me—pace, boundaries and what commentators call 'anchor points'. If I find the pace getting too rushed, I have to actively remind myself to slow down and vice versa. Boundaries are more like guidelines rather than limitations. They include starting or ending the day with exercise, having dinner with the children, ending the evening with a relaxing activity, not going out at night more than twice a week, not working after dinner—all intended to help me sleep better.

Psychologists Steven Jones, Peter Hayward and Dominic Lam mention 'anchor points' in their book *Coping with Bipolar Disorder: A CBT-informed Guide to Living with Manic Depression.* I found it a useful concept. A routine does not imply that one should do things at exactly the same time, they say. For example, 'with eating it is beneficial that there are three eating periods in the day and that these are at the beginning of the day, somewhere in the middle of the day, and then towards the end of the day. It is the presence of these "anchor points" that is important rather than the precise time at which they occur,'[1] they write. They help in establishing a 'protective' routine, one that is supportive during the cycles.

Lifestyle therapy is my term for maintaining a healthy rhythm of the day. In practical terms, it comprises three main 'anchor points', according to me: sleep, exercise and nutrition. These are obvious candidates for a healthy lifestyle for anyone, so I will just elaborate on their role in the context of bipolarity and mental health, more than anything else.

● ● ●

Anchor Point 1: Sleep Is the Key to Bipolar Nirvana

April 2021, Mumbai

It is evening and I'm trying to cope with Covid-related anxiety, hoping for a good night's sleep. My doctor has given me a light sleeping aid. I turn to a curated set of pre-bedtime rituals to enable me to sleep, such as reading, watching Netflix, playing the piano, chatting with friends and family, persuading a member of the family to give me a quick back rub and listening to guided deep relaxation and yoga nidra practices.

Sleep is the key to bipolar nirvana, as far as I'm concerned. Without sleep deprivation, there is no bipolar disorder. Getting a good night's sleep is vital to avoid getting into a manic episode. Restlessness at night is a symptom of the fact that my mind is troubled. Sooner or later, it will implode, with undesirable consequences. I recall, with dread, going through weeks of truncated sleep, and am learning to be vigilant about its triggers and red flags—whether stress, anxiety, excitement, interpersonal conflict or anything else.

The experts are unanimous on the relationship between bipolarity and sleep. 'Sleep restores, reboots, it helps with regeneration of damaged cells in the body, it resets hormonal imbalances, it gives your brain a rest, it's very, very critical,' says my psychiatrist Dr Zirak Marker.

'Decreased sleep is both a symptom of mania and a cause,'[2] writes Kay Redfield Jamison in her memoir, *An Unquiet Mind.*

'There is no major psychiatric condition in which sleep is normal. This is true of depression, anxiety, post-traumatic stress disorder (PTSD), schizophrenia and bipolar disorder . . . many of the brain regions commonly involved with psychiatric mood disorders are the same regions that are involved in sleep regulation and impacted by sleep loss. Further, many of the genes that show abnormalities in psychiatric illnesses are the same genes that help control sleep and our circadian rhythm,'[3] explains Matthew Walker in *Why We Sleep: The New Science of Sleep and Dreams.*

He describes sleep loss and mental illness as a 'two-way street of interaction, with the flow of traffic being stronger in one direction or the other, depending on the disorder.'[4]

● ● ●

Anchor Point 2: Calibrate Exercise to Suit the Mood

January 2021, Mumbai

'Faster, faster, where is the speed? Come on champion, come on buddy,' urges my personal trainer Harish Shetty as he persuades me to push myself with a mix of coercion and humour. It is early evening, and I am in the gym. Our regime varies between strength and endurance training to keep the workouts challenging in intensity. I have to motivate myself for the class before we begin, preparing myself to be physically tested.

Exercise is the second pillar, and it is as much of a religion as good sleep. It helps me maintain equilibrium on normal days; it helps me come down from a manic high; it makes it easier to cope when feeling stressed or anxious and picks me up when I'm feeling down. As I mentioned, walking, yoga and personal training have largely comprised my exercise regime. Walking regulates my thoughts in a peaceful way, even if it's just a stroll. My yoga teacher Rajesh Shelar calibrates the lesson depending on my mood and energy levels, with gentle stretching on days when I have not slept properly and more demanding asanas and kickboxing when I am more rested. And I trained for many years with a trainer named Shilpa Rane, and then for the last three years with Harish Shetty. Personal trainers promote discipline but, in their absence, there are many options today—group classes, apps and online videos.

'A good session of exercise helps you to sleep better, helps cognitive functions, better memory, better coordination, better hormonal balance, promotes fat loss and muscle gain, gives you a neurotransmitter boost. If any of these are out of whack, we have a problem. So exercise is going to help anyone with a mental health condition to overcome it and cope better,' says Harish.

Differences in my energy levels are visible during training. 'In the morning, you're not so charged up, you take a little more time to start your engine. You finish your warm-up, do a few sets and that's when you kind of wake up. In the evening, it's completely the opposite, you're there from the word go. Sometimes there are days when you're not fully there, so I will do something which will probably take us longer to reach what we plan to, or we do something completely different, which will make you feel better. At the end of the day, the goal is that when you step out of the gym, it has to be on a positive note. So we've been constantly changing when the energy level has been low.'

'Your strength and fitness have definitely improved from when we started, and you're very self-motivated, which is your biggest strength. I would love to see you run more and to see you squat with at least 135 pounds because I feel you have the strength but there's some fear, maybe of injury,' says Harish.

My current nutritionist Kinita Kadakia Patel, who is also a sports nutritionist, feels that those who exercise cheat less on a diet. 'A diet gets restrictive but the sense of achievement that exercise gives doesn't want you to cheat. So there's a good combination.'

Anchor Point 3: Retain Optimism about Nutrition and Weight Loss, Even When Progress Is Glacial

Which brings me to the third pillar, nutrition. Despite a regular exercise regime and the attention to nutrition and diet, weight loss has been elusive. Medicines have definitely been responsible, as I gained fifteen kilos after starting them, but the mood swings don't help either. My dietary intake increases during my ups and downs, making it harder to shift the weight when I am at equilibrium. I have lost anywhere from five to twelve kilos when I am stable, only to regain them during back-to-back mood swings. Reclaiming my body has been harder for me than reclaiming my mind. My journal shows a consistent pattern of entries over the years.

20 December 2016

Weight loss—I need to put this on top of my wish list for 2017. I feel I've put on weight after going on antipsychotics in August.

18 December 2017

Too many shadow comforts . . . diet and exercise need to be reclaimed in a big way!

31 January 2021

Why am I still so heavy despite all my efforts—counting calories, gym workouts, giving up sugar, bread, dahi. How can I live a full life, the life I want to lead—Soho, friends, work and its associated outings—and still lose weight? Why do I find it so difficult to wake up in the morning and work out? Why can't I walk faster and increase my metabolic rate? Why can't I limit myself when eating out? Why, why, why?

31 August 2021

A disheartening start to the day, I'm now 3 kilos up since May instead of 12 kilos down. Eating out, sugar, lack of portion control and appetite are the culprits. I feel I've been on a diet that not's been working for most of my adult life. And especially for the last 6–7 years. Like I've been living mentally with deprivation and then cheating, rather than being free to eat what I want to. Sigh deeply and find a solution.

I've been to half a dozen nutritionists and a psychologist over the years for weight loss and fat loss. Two individuals who have worked closely with me during my mood swings are Tara Mahadevan and Kinita. Both have observed how food becomes comforting—a feel-good factor—during mood swings.

'You struggled with cycling between depression and mania and physically that is exhausting, there is no stability for the body. The medications alter your physiology, your metabolism, your energy levels, your sleep. So when all of these physiological systems don't have any stability, then the need to want more food, and crave more sweets, just becomes heightened. So it's not out of greed or laziness, or because you just love food that much, it's because partly you're seeking some kind of stability, and you need that energy. Your journey to maintaining a healthy weight looks very different from someone who does not take those same medications, at the same level, and who does not have those same cycles. It's that much tougher for you,' says Tara.

She talked to me about 'breathing out emotions and not eating them in. The more we are connected to and aware of our emotions, the less we feel the need to use food to soothe ourselves or to pass the time. When we have a healthy relationship with our emotions, a healthier relationship with food sorts itself out,' she says.

Mindful eating is Tara's preferred technique for weight loss. 'Recognizing when we are eating for physical hunger and when for emotional hunger. If eating becomes the only way to deal with our emotional hunger, that is something to be addressed. A big part of mindful eating is also eating with full presence, without distraction. So not eating in front of a television or a computer, or while reading,' for example, she says, adding 'you have a very sharp mind, you have a mind that thinks a lot, that has lots of different creative ideas. And sometimes you would eat while you were thinking, and that became another kind of mindless eating,' she observes. So much of bipolarity is about acting on impulse, and this extends to food. I can be impulsive about snacks, desserts or an extra portion size—the opposite of mindful eating.

I went to Tara regularly for over a year between 2014 and 2016 and was close to reaching my ideal weight. I then decided to take a break, but I regained the weight I'd lost, when my gynaecologist recommended Kinita to me in late 2017. I've been going to her since then, with a longish break in between.

November 2017, Mumbai

Kinita and I are in her clinic. The weighing scale lies to our side, unmoving, unchanging, unrelenting. Today, we don't discuss the diet at all, and I tell her what's on my mind. It is a longer meeting than normal.

Kinita meets her clients every week, with a weekly customized diet plan and a weigh-in to monitor weight loss. She advocates a 'meal pyramid', consisting of macronutrients at the base, with micronutrients one level up and finally supplements. 'Macronutrients are the big chunks that we eat in the day, the carbohydrates, the protein, the fat. Getting the right combination of these three is critical as a part of my pyramid. I am not a believer of withdrawal of any one of them completely. I work very closely on a weekly basis, or on a much more individualized basis, to curate these ratios which are effective, and then I work on micros, which are magnesium, selenium, calcium, vitamins, minerals. These are what make the macros complete. And then I go on to any kind of supplements, my supplements are more for athletes, who work very closely with injuries and recovery,' she explains.

My moods drive the weekly diet plan, she says. 'When dealing with mental health conditions, there are phases and triggers. You might have a trigger one week, and you're completely out of your skin and anxious and you're getting a panic attack. I cannot put you on a diet. But you might have a beautiful week the next week, and you are full of energy and you're feeling great. We work on stronger diets at that time. So I have to create this balance. I find the journey much more stable now, you are much more in control and in sync with what you are eating. The number of bad days is less than earlier.

'You've actually been one of those cases that have honestly not been very difficult. Because as many bad days as you have had, you have always allowed yourself to get up and say, "Okay, now I'm ready to do this diet" or you have been in complete understanding of your phase and said, "You know what, I need few days off", which a lot of people don't know. And that's been my strategy with you, whenever you've taken off, we've come back, we've gone with a vengeance on a diet, and we have done low carb diets, we have done high protein diets, and we've got great results. Many times we've said, "Okay, let's take a break, and then we'll revisit this after a few weeks once you are in a better space".

'And with you, I have noticed that holidays always worked. You always got in a better space when you came back. And then something would go off, and a few weeks would be a little bit stressful with food. And in those few weeks, I never used to withdraw carbs. That has always been my strategy. I've tried to keep the diet as wholesome as possible. I have always asked you, "What do you want in life? What is it that you are craving? Is there anything you want me to add in the diet?" And then if there was an answer, I have worked the diet the other way around, keeping what you want in the diet. So that's been a key strategy that I have worked with, by knowing what you want. And then working my diet around rather than me telling you what you need to eat.'

I retain my optimism, despite the glacial pace of progress, that's all I can say (Although sadly glaciers seem to move faster than my weighing scale, with climate change).

I will end this section with a postscript—until now I have always thought that the gut mirrors my emotions and moods, that my emotions are played out in my stomach. But Dr Emeran Mayer, an eminent gastroenterologist and pioneering researcher in the area of brain-gut interactions, suggests that the relationship between the two is more intricate. Author of *The Mind-Gut Connection: How the Hidden Conversation Within Our Bodies Impacts Our Mood, Our Choices and Our Overall Health*, he writes that scientific data 'suggest that the microbiota in our gut play a critical role in the complex interactions between mind, brain and gut. This exciting line of research has inspired paradigm-breaking ideas regarding the role of these invisible creatures in our gut reactions and gut feelings, and how they might affect our moods, minds and thoughts . . . I strongly feel that it is the engagement of the gut and its microbiome that plays a major role in determining the intensity, duration and uniqueness of our emotional feelings.'[5] Another important reason to focus on gut health.

● ● ●

This triple prescription for wellness might result in balance, but does it necessitate military-like discipline? How do I find the daily routine to be a source of comfort and peace and not a constraint?

The answer lies in another key element of lifestyle therapy, which to me is just as important as sleep, exercise and nutrition: playfulness, irreverence and humour. They add joy to everyday life.

May 2021, Mumbai

It is the second lockdown. Amartya and I try to defeat each other daily at an epic board game, 'Wildlife Adventure', which was popular when Radhika and I were young, while Agastya hovers over us, trying to get us to reinvent the rules of the game.

Having two children enlivens the day like nothing else. 'Wildlife Adventure' is just one example—playing table-tennis with both boys, discussing Lego with Agastya or playing family hide-and-seek at night are other ways of having fun, every day. Agastya loves to corral us into playing 'Skribbl', an online version of 'Pictionary', where our family in London also join in.

'The truth is that in most cases, play is a catalyst. The beneficial effects of getting just a little true play can spread throughout our lives, actually making us more productive and happier in everything we do,'[6] writes Dr Stuart Brown. A doctor, a psychiatrist and a clinical researcher, Brown is the author, along with writer Christopher Vaughan, of *Play: How It Shapes the Brain, Opens the Imagination, and Invigorates the Soul.* 'Play is the vital essence of life. It is what make life lively,' he says, adding it is 'a force that allows us to both discover our most essential selves and enlarge our world. We are designed to find fulfilment and creative growth through play.'[7]

Solo play is just as fun as shared games. I've been inconsistent with keeping up childhood hobbies, but I'm trying to get back to riding in particular. Riding represents adventure and excitement, unlike any other. Reading, whether novels or non-fiction, is essential, as is Netflix. Art and culture channel and absorb emotion. In pre-Covid days (and post-Covid days I hope), the Asia Society, literature festivals and Shanmukhananda Hall were favourite haunts.

And then there's listening to music. One anecdote that I think could help anyone suffering from depression is music-related. Amartya learnt a number of 'motivational' pop songs in his Western music class at school. So I made a playlist of all the motivational songs that he was learning (some of which I knew but had forgotten) and called it 'Think Positive'. It helped me a lot during moments of depression and continues to motivate me. (Yes, the playlist is quite sentimental, and it includes Mariah Carey's 'Hero', an indication of just how middle-aged I am. My twenty-year-old self would not be impressed with my music choice. But it worked! I've listened to 'Hero' dozens of times!)

Yet I have to be careful with music because it can be as much of a trigger as a source of meditative calm. Every self-respecting manic episode has a music soundtrack. To begin with, bhajans and spiritual music to find solace—and sleep—during the late nights and early mornings. But I soon veer to others, for example, 'Dum Maro Dum', 'Chitta Ve', 'Udta Punjab or 'Beedi' on repeat, walking round and round my building with mounting adrenaline. I've learnt to recognize that these same songs serve as warning signs. If I'm listening to them more than once, it's time to switch to something innocuous, like 'Desi Girl'.

Those days are becoming rarer. Now, most days I'll listen to music in the car or during my walks, ranging from pop and rock to Bollywood, spiritual music and cheesy Abba playlists. One of my most special moments was when the boys were young, and we were driving back home from a dinner. They were nearly falling asleep in their car seats on either side of me, and we were listening to 'Achyutam Keshavam'. The melody—and the silence between songs—was so peaceful.

Play, to me, is also as much about attitude as it is about activity, about unlocking one's irreverent, light-hearted, humorous side. A few years ago, I sent out this message:

I'm a year older on Sunday and if there's one thing I'd like to attempt to reclaim, it's a measure of spontaneity! Amit and I would love it if you could rejig whatever can be rejigged in your schedule, and if you and yours can join us for a leisurely Sunday brunch at home. Please do RSVP. Aparna

Fifty friends showed up at three days' notice! I would like to think that I can maintain this levity.

All these aspects of lifestyle therapy help with trigger management, shifting attention from whatever is causing the stress and focusing on everyday simplicity, alongside work and family responsibilities. One day at a time.

I would like to end with a piece that I think speaks for itself, written a year after we moved into our new home.

Aches and Grins

Whenever I am sad and blue
Whenever I am dull and slow
I know you will be there for me

A ray of sunlight
On every rainy, dusty or smog-filled morning
Almost nearly 24/7

Always happy for me to open the door
You will make sure

I'm calm and relaxed
Or laughing and playful
Or wet and sweaty

My one and only . . . clubhouse
Yoga, boot camp, badminton, gym

With multiple, middle-aged mammas
Negotiating with obstinate body parts

A daily diet for many aches, even more grins.

Part III: Conclusion

I have come to realize that the stronger you are, the more hurt you can handle. And the less you share that hurt with anyone, the more the accumulated emotion.

I've experienced every possible negative emotion—anger, frustration, resentment, fear and paranoia. It has made me volatile, manic, uncontrollable, deluded, sleep-deprived and generally a pain to handle.

But from that has emerged so much that's good about my life: truth, compassion, wisdom, patience and most of all, love. Could I live without being bipolar? Absolutely. And my family would echo that ten-times over. But it has provided me the opportunity to examine my life like no other.

30 August 2016
(extract from journal)

11

Reflections on Mental Health

23 July 2021

Back from a week in Goa, to my favourite Soho House, and the first thought that comes to my mind as I reflect on this manuscript: I did it. I've written it. To all those who said: 'don't write on mental health, don't publish a memoir, don't write on urbanization, don't write a screenplay'—well, here it is. Over 70,000 words on losing (and healing) my mind, while staying sane. I want to savour this moment.

So how do I feel about being bipolar? About mental health? About my book? I've tried to assemble a few realizations and memorable quotes from friends, family and mentors. For every reader who made it this far, and for those who might be picking it up from the end, here's a listicle to keep things simple. Not a summary of each chapter, but themes that I hope run through the book:

1. **Living with vulnerability is about accepting the difference between personality and illness and learning to love both. Bipolarity is a struggle but it was illuminating once I accepted it.**

Yes, I have an illness. Bipolarity is complicated. One psychiatrist I spoke with describes it as 'one of the most complex conditions diagnostically, because you see so much variation. It has a unique role in psychiatry because it's such an interesting and devastating condition. In so many instances, it has severe depression, psychosis, insomnia. It's the only condition where all of these things are present. Just the heterogeneity is so immense.'

These extremes are isolated occurrences in my case, at least these days. But mood swings are constant companions. In a given week, I can be all seven colours of the rainbow. I try and observe my emotions, not become them. They do not define me. My personality is reflected in how I respond to my illness, not by my illness itself. I can act. I can shape my moods. I can change my environment when I'm down so I'm not tethered to my bed. Home can be a warm glow but it can also be a cave of my depression. I can exhale and say thanks when I'm having a good day, just rejoicing in the moment and pacing myself.

My friend Seema Bhangar's comments are always reassuring in this regard. She is such a great daily download friend, who knows my everyday battles to stay afloat. 'It's really hard. I had not appreciated it before. As your friend, I enjoy the fruits of your internal struggles and see a coherent and high-functioning exterior without seeing (until you tell me) just how hard it is to live with your mind. You are wise to make time and space for it, and to prioritize its health (via the right doses of sleep, solitude and the other almost-formulaic things you know it needs, especially during external instability and transition). This willingness to start being kind to yourself came through as a key part of the journey. Almost with the kind of fierceness we bring to protecting and caring for our children, which makes sense, because this is in a way your child within.'

My first psychotherapist, Radhika Sheth, also interprets what others might see as my vulnerabilities—my untamed mind—as my 'free child, an uncensored person that doesn't have any rights and wrongs, but just runs towards pleasure, without thinking of the consequences. I think it was a very powerful part of you, which you found a way to express. To be able to access that free child, to be able to laugh, to be humorous, to engage people in that free child, is to be very life-giving,' she feels.

That's a comforting perspective, but of course I know I should leverage that inner child to fruitful ends. Perhaps the biggest gift that bipolarity has bestowed on me is the opportunity for self-examination, something that might not have happened if I didn't have a mental health condition. Our Vedanta teacher shared a wonderful quote in class. 'It is difficult to find happiness within oneself, but it is impossible to find it anywhere else.' The self is the source of the happiness you are seeking outside. Your true nature, he said, is a state of complete, unbroken, infinite, eternal peace, bliss, contentment. Another way of putting it—to be happy for no reason.

So my biggest hope for this book is that it will help readers reframe how they look at vulnerabilities and be more open in sharing them. Whenever I mention mental health to anyone, without fail, they reveal a similar story of someone in their immediate circle. Or they might disclose a physical vulnerability—having to take heart medication in their forties or getting used to a hearing aid early in their fifties.

After a certain age, most of us live with ailments of differing magnitudes of seriousness. Maybe we can be kinder, and more accepting, of ourselves, and of each other, in how to react to each other's vulnerabilities, and our own.

2. **The seven therapies are universal and they are complementary.**

This book is about mental health in the context of bipolarity, but I believe that this therapy tree applies to everyone, not just those who are bipolar (and, in fact, not just those who have a mental health condition). Dr Raman, our close family friend and a leading cancer surgeon, validates my thought. 'Health is defined as "physical, mental, social and spiritual well-being". Your seven therapies are absolutely essential if one wishes to address any illness, be it mental or physical, in a holistic way and meet these parameters. You are absolutely right in saying that these therapies could and should be tried universally for all beyond those with mental stress,' he says, adding that he follows this holistic approach in his clinics and hospitals too.

I would also like to think that the therapies complement each other, instead of pulling the reader in opposite directions. For example, the seemingly contrary approaches of spirituality and medical therapies can harmonize. Work therapy and lifestyle therapy together can foster equilibrium rather than igniting stress. And family and friends can form partnerships to promote recovery and healing.

3. **Mental health is a team sport.**

I also hope the book reiterates the massive role of community, defined in its widest, and most positive, sense. If I've learnt anything, it's that meds will never be enough. My tribe of 'therapists' represent the valuable roles that all stakeholders play in promoting any individual's mental health and wellness. As I said earlier, if it takes a village to raise a child, it takes a community of allies to heal a mind. And support doesn't always need to be in big ways, or in medical emergencies. One of the most helpful communities in my life is the Vivarea building WhatsApp group—better than Google at locating information or last-minute resources, as we often say! The group members' support is unequivocal, whether they know that I'm bipolar or not.

4. **Unburdening guilt and realizing that everyone needs looking after.**

Nobody wants to be a burden on their family. I've been extraordinarily lucky with my caregivers, but the situation is changing, I am much more of a caregiver to my family myself now. Mom is getting older, Radhika and Amanda live thousands of miles away, Amit has a demanding job; despite their best intentions they may not be in a position to help as much as in the past. The children are more perceptive, and I don't want them turning into my caregivers.

So I would like my readers to understand that a mental health condition need not leave one overwhelmed with guilt. When I had my first manic episodes, there were 'whispers' questioning how I would get married, declaring that kids were out of the question. Yet here we are, two decades later. Being a mother is, in fact, one part of my life where I don't need external validation. Sure, I have had to retreat on more than one occasion to my mother's or sister's home. Equally, I do all the tasks and activities parents do, from the routine vaccinations, dental check-ups and parent-teacher meetings to the fun stuff such as organizing birthday parties, play dates and holidays. Both boys are happy, secure and confident, and young enough to love their parents. Agastya still asks for me when I'm out writing at Soho House. 'Mamma is kind and caring, we have lunch together every day, she and I plan my birthday parties and play dates, and she buys me Lego,' he says.

A recent conversation with Amartya says it all. We were watching a test match on TV when I spotted a woman in the audience holding a placard with 'no cricket, no life' written on it. The Indian tricolour was painted on both her cheeks.

Aparna: You need a mom like that.
Amartya: No, I like this one. (Hugs me).

They are—indescribable. My loves.

Amit characterizes the relationship between bipolarity, motherhood and caregiving with a humorous reference to his favourite pastime these days, equity investing. 'I have been hugely influenced by Warren Buffett and Charlie Munger's writing and speeches. At the 2007 Berkshire Hathaway annual meeting, Mr Buffett made an iconic statement. While it was made in the context of investing, I believe that there is a far deeper meaning to it. He said, "Volatility is not a measure of risk".[1] He goes on to explain rather eloquently that past volatility in stock prices does not determine the risk of business. Business risk is determined by many factors such as leverage (debt), the business losing competitive advantage, etc.'

'During 2013 to 2018, Aparna had recurrent episodes, when her behaviour was erratic and volatile. I constantly worried about the potential psychological impact on the kids. But over the years, I have strongly come to believe that there has not been any impact on the kids' psyche. Of course, there will be many other things that will shape their psychological architecture, but definitely not Aparna's episodes,' Amit says.

'During episodes and during the calmer periods, Aparna remains a fantastic, loving mother. She has significantly shaped the kids' personalities by encouraging them to have an enquiring mind and exploring different activities and interests. At the core, during calmer and volatile periods, she never lost her maternal instincts and never put the kids at risk (except once). So if I were to relate Mr Buffett's statement to our condition, Aparna's volatility had nothing to do with how good or bad she was as a mother. She never put the kids at risk, and hence she is a great mother. I had to weather the volatility as I was convinced that the underlying asset was great!' he says.

Nice to be compared to a strong-performing stock! The fact remains—I am the primary caregiver to this family. And caregivers need help too, from time to time, when they are unwell. There's nothing to feel guilty, ashamed or embarrassed about.

5. **Rediscovering agency, not looking at myself as a victim, and learning to live to my full potential.**

I have an illness, but I am not unwell, not every day at least. My condition does not stop me from living to my fullest potential. This is one of my most fundamental realizations, and I hope a theme that will resonate with readers. One of my favourite anecdotes is a conversation with my HBS classmate Michelle. It was a few years ago, and I had known her for over a decade at the time. As a strategic consultant to the pharmaceutical industry, she is pretty well acquainted with medical conditions. We were chatting over an HBS women's alumni dinner, and I said that I was working on a book about being bipolar.

> Michelle: Who is bipolar?
> Aparna: I am.
> Michelle (two minutes later): Are you sure? I've never sensed it.
> Aparna: Yes.
> Michelle: It's very well managed, then.

'It's very well managed.' And that's what it is: something manageable and liveable, not a terrifying life-sentence.

Coping and surviving are essential elements of mental wellness, but insufficient on their own. Mental wellness is about fulfilling one's potential—in all its dimensions. Healing oneself emotionally, psychologically, spiritually, physically, financially. Living a full life is important for me; it fuels my resilience. I've spoken about many of these aspects of well-being in the book already; one important criterion I would like to touch upon is independence and agency.

I felt I had more of both two decades ago when I was in my twenties, especially when it comes to travel, than I do now. I learnt how to scuba-dive, volunteered to build a school in the heart of the Amazonian rainforest, went on a budget camping safari in Tanzania and heard lions roar at night—without really having to take anyone's permission to do so. Of course, as a mother of two schoolchildren, I can't just take off and travel to offbeat remote locations at short notice, but I do want to regain some of the independence I had as a young adult. The domestic cocoon—coupled with the mental health condition—can easily turn into a crutch. Just as stability is the most obvious mental health goal, and I strive to increase the intervals between my manic episodes, the prospect of more frequent travel to exciting locations is a huge motivation to remain peaceful.

6. **A post-Covid realization: mental health can be managed remotely—and globally.**

Earlier, I would associate being bipolar with memories of being taken to my psychiatrist's clinic when I was manic and being put on heavyweight antipsychotics. Someone (my family and maybe a friend) would need to take me there and back. In other words, this would be an in-person interaction, an in-person diagnosis and prescription, followed up by in-person counselling.

But now, that scenario has changed. I am much more aware of my red flags, so even, potentially volatile situations have not escalated over the last four years to mania or hypomania. Many of the therapies keeping me stable every day are 'offline'—spending time with my immediate family, going to the gym or Soho House, meeting my friends, advising a Mumbai-based non-profit. But just as many of them are daily, virtual exchanges: Radhika, Amanda and Dr Shanahan live in London, my two closest friends live in Dubai and San Francisco, my work colleagues are distributed between Delhi, Hyderabad and Ahmedabad. Because of Covid, even the in-person interactions with a Mumbai-based mentor such as Khozem have become digital.

So what I have now realized is that just like other aspects of health, mental health, at least in this urban setting, can be managed remotely, from anywhere in the world. And to those who might be placed at a distance and wonder how they can help a loved one with a mental health condition, my suggestion is simple: stay connected and be responsive! Be in sync! Via video calls, messaging or voice notes. That's all it takes.

7. Playing opposite-handed.

This metaphor informs my work life. For someone who can get stressed with too much work and depressed with too little, playing opposite-handed allows me to exist within this narrow bandwidth of desired professional ambition and actual professional ability. Playing opposite-handed means learning to work as if I were playing a sport with my opposite hand: slower, more mindfully, with more breaks between shots. This might seem unnatural at first, but I find it is more sustainable. In other words, I need to adopt the opposite behaviour of my natural instincts if I want to cope with bipolarity without sacrificing my ambitions.

As I said earlier, playing opposite-handed has become the bedrock of my approach to work. I pursue many activities, but only a little bit at a time. Whether it's writing books or a column, teaching, speaking or advising, I usually have flexibility and control on the pace and the intensity of my work. This allows me to adjust my schedule if I'm feeling tired, stressed or overwhelmed.

8. Attending to the garden of mental health—every day matters.

Joint pain can be ignored, even earaches can be tolerated but, as my friend Mary says, mental health and well-being is a garden that needs tending to daily. It will start drooping if it is neglected even for a day and needs urgent attention in case of pest invasion.

Lifestyle therapy, in the form of sleep, exercise, nutrition, and also playfulness and humour are essential in tending to this garden to keep it blooming. Other daily practices—chatting with friends, meditation through music, some alone time—are all ways I try and keep this garden in good shape, whatever the weather.

9. **Discovering the meaning of success, happiness and fulfilment.**

If that sounds like a book in itself, it probably is, because it is one of the recurring themes of this book. The desire for professional success was one of the most persistent triggers for mood swings, and it was entwined with my sense of self and identity. As I wrote in my journal in January 2015:

> Successful, so what?
> I still haven't reached the stage where I can completely question or forfeit success entirely. I can define it more narrowly, meaningfully and lower the bar. I can't get myself to forfeit it or to completely take my eye away from it, even though I know all success is temporal and often marginal in its ultimate value.

At some point over the years I came to disassociate my identity with professional success, as Radhika Sheth reminds me. 'I think for you, the energies were more on the scale of wanting to do and to prove, rather than just allowing yourself to be, and I think that balance was required between to do and to be, between being and doing. It was about working and achieving and still being a mother and a wife, and whatever are the softer parts of femininity, and the more powerful and achieving and proving parts. I think that was where you probably found a balance for yourself.'

I also learnt to disentangle happiness from the manic highs. It was a hard feeling to jettison. But in December 2016 I crafted an alternative definition of fulfilment for myself and began to realize that personal happiness is more important than what I might have expected it to be two decades ago, and that it preceded professional success, as I wrote in my journal on 20 December 2016:

> What is fulfilment? For me fulfilment lay in understanding many important intangibles in life: happiness and success (knowing which comes first), purpose (getting closer to understanding it), love (always important), fantasy and ego (understanding the connections and letting go of them), giving and sharing (doing more of both), the joy of creativity (without the grandiosity), interpersonal relationships (without conflict) and the simple rhythm of life (adopting it).

To that I would add: adventure (whether on a horse or in a remote location, or preferably both), solitude (in any quantity) and nature (my true oxygen). Many of the above elements have appeared in the book already, so I would like to take a few minutes to dwell on those that haven't been featured very much—adventure, nature and travel.

Sometimes I wonder what stops me from getting back in the saddle when I love horse riding so much. Maybe it's because I feel like a sack of potatoes on a horse right now and that I need some lessons to feel comfortable again. All I know is I want to be able to gallop in Shekhawati in Rajasthan on a horse safari with Rads. Nature, the outdoors, adventure— all bound up in one dream trip. My preoccupation with professional accomplishments has occupied so many pages of this book—and they are legitimate concerns—but personally, few things make me happier and more fulfilled than travel. And not to cities but to be a part of nature: preferably mountains, forests, hills, deserts. Biophilia is as much a part of my genetic make-up as bipolarity.

10. 'Life's a journey, not a destination.'

This proverb, often attributed to poet Ralph Waldo Emerson, is clichéd, but so true. The rock band Aerosmith included it in one of my favourite songs, 'Amazing' and added the line: 'And you just can't tell what tomorrow brings', which is even truer. One day I can be content and happy after a wholesome nature walk, and the next day I'm obsessing about book marketing and my woeful number of Instagram followers.

Bipolarity can seem like a recurring cycle, a pendulum, or a roller coaster, but above all, it is a journey. Maintaining balance, seeking happiness and fulfilment and expanding my sense of agency are my milestones for the next stage of this journey. Arriving at these milestones has been an expedition in itself, with the seven therapies as my wayfinding signposts.

11. The importance of having conversations with yourself.

The last realization I would love for a reader to take away is the importance of spending time with yourself to reflect on thoughts or emotions, to gain insights into one's triggers or to find new meaning in everyday existence.

My friend Mary observes that my self-therapy seems to be working. 'I feel like there was a time when you rode the ups and downs a little bit more. Now I would almost say you have a more detached relationship with it, you can observe this cycle and recognize it and deal with it now in a different way than maybe you used to. So maybe you've learnt to live with it.'

Frustrations abound, nevertheless. Negative thoughts, such as fears and anxieties, plague me often. My mind visualizes situations escalating into unreasonable calamities, a practice that Dr Zirak refers to as 'catastrophizing'. I need to summon all the force of my intellect to refute these scenarios and, even then, I don't always succeed. I read a quote, 'the best use of imagination is creativity, the worst use of imagination is anxiety', attributed to the alternative medicine advocate and author, Deepak Chopra. It resonated like a loud gong in my brain!

I still do not know why I am destined to experience emotion with so much intensity, why my inner world is often filled with so much heat and light. I have learnt that suppressing feelings underground is as lethal as giving them too much oxygen or daylight.

In my most optimistic moments, I like to believe I am made this way because I am capable of harnessing these terrifyingly creative energies, of producing something as brilliant as the spark that often threatens my stability. Even if that does not turn out to be true, I know that living with this condition has brought me closer to personal illumination, for which I feel blessed, grateful and most of all, loved.

That's about it for me. What next for the reader or the caregiver who might be dealing with a (possibly undiagnosed) mental health condition? Here are my suggestions for starters:

1. Know that you are not alone. Talk to a friend, a family member, maybe a co-worker about your thoughts and emotions. Keep an open mind to taking their advice.

2. Try out the self-care apps listed at the end of the book.
3. If you feel ready to speak with a mental health professional, consider accessing some of the resources listed in the same section.
4. Listen to your body. When I need to nap in the afternoons (or after breakfast), I do.
5. Exercise regularly—it could be a walk, yoga, gym or whatever you prefer.
6. Spend some time in nature. The sea, beach, mountains, hills, public parks, or just in sunlight, whatever is available and accessible.
7. Start writing a journal, documenting your thoughts and feelings.
8. And if you can include everything that you're grateful for, that would be ideal!
9. Be kind to yourself. It always helps. I find adjusting my expectations of myself is a good start.
10. Connect with me. Find me on social media or visit my website. I'll do my best to respond.

My final poem is about managing emotions and was inspired by the courage shown by two friends on the tragic, untimely and unexpected deaths of their husbands.

Waterfall

You are my waterfall
I am your spectator
I marvel at your roar
Without getting drenched
By your deluge

You are my desert
Stark, empty, endless

I observe your horizon
But do not dissolve in your solitude
I know the horizon is
'Merely the limit of my sight'.

You are my most ancient tree
I lie in your shadow
Gaze up at your gnarled branches,
Knowing I cannot alter your asymmetry.
Branches must grow in different directions

You are my emotions
Precious and beautiful
Overwhelming and bleak

You are mine
But you are not me.

More fleeting than childhood,
I know you must leave
Without any permanent residue.

More fleeting than childhood,
I know you will leave
And fortify me
With 'gratitude, perseverance, and hope'
My diyas for inner lightness.

12

Future Therapies

W hy stop at seven therapies? In my search for thinkers
and doers in mental healthcare, I came across five
individuals who are doing fascinating work in mental
health. They differ greatly in their backgrounds, roles and
occupations. Yet together, they reframe how we could—and
should—think of mental health. This line of thinking is the
basis of future therapies, according to me.

Dr Alex Charney, New York
Dr Shebani Sethi Dalai, Palo Alto
Narendra Kinger, Mumbai
Dr Soumitra Pathare, Pune
Raj Mariwala, Mumbai

Let's start with Alex. A physician-scientist specializing in
the neurobiology of neuropsychiatric illness, he is a data
scientist on genetic studies of schizophrenia and bipolar
disorder and plays a lead role in several of the largest studies
in the field of psychiatric genomics.

*Dr Alex Charney has a colourful print of nerve cells behind
him. I see it through my laptop camera. It was given to him by*

a former labmate and a scientist-artist, he tells me. A geneticist, psychiatrist and neuroscientist at the globally renowned Mount Sinai group of hospitals in New York, Alex shares the latest progress in the genetics of psychiatric illnesses.

I am curious to know about the genetics of psychiatric illness, to understand the origins of the condition and its prospects for future drug therapies. Alex simplifies the field for a layperson such as myself. Back in the 1980s and 1990s, scientists assumed there was a single gene for many psychiatric conditions, whether mania, depression or schizophrenia. But over time, that premise was proved wrong, resulting in a 'paradigm shift in the way studies were done'. The new assumption was that 'the entire genome of an individual kind of predisposes them to be at risk for a condition,' he says. Modern technology facilitated genome-wide association studies, supporting this hypothesis. 'Now we find ourselves in a place where we have really good, robust replicated findings that point us in the right direction. The key nuance is that there is no single gene that makes a huge contribution,' he says. Instead, there are many areas of the genome that contribute a little bit to one's risk of illness.

'Importantly, these areas of the genome are not like rare "mutations", changing someone's genome to give them bipolar disorder. These are genetic variants that everyone has. It's not like something goes wrong in the genome. But if you carry the wrong combination, or an unlucky combination, or you have a few too many of these variants in the wrong environmental setting (I'm hypothesizing here, we don't know exactly how it happens), you could develop bipolar disorder, for example,' he explains.

The other finding is that 'at the genetic level, conditions such as schizophrenia, bipolar disorder and depression are very overlapping. The genetic variants that contribute to your risk are not distinct from one condition to another, necessarily,' Alex says.

Bipolar disorder is extremely heritable, he tells me. The chances that I inherited it from a family member are high, which makes me feel guilty. What if I pass it on to my children? Counter-intuitive as it might sound, the probability is low, approximately 10 per cent, Alex says. It is a higher probability than for someone with no history of bipolarity in the family, but still a low probability.

My next question relates to future drug therapies. Does all this insight into the genetics of bipolar disorder translate into new drug therapies? 'This is a problem for the field. There are hundreds of genes that we've now statistically linked to this condition. And, as we said, none of them contributes a lot, they each have a small effect. And they're interacting in a way we don't understand, so it becomes very difficult neurobiologically to understand what this means,' Alex acknowledges. 'As our knowledge of genetics has skyrocketed, the number of drug trials has gone down. Our knowledge of the complexity has led to the field being somewhat paralysed, because if you are going to invest a billion dollars in developing a new treatment based on a specific target, you want to be confident that it targets the right one.' Even more reason to emphasize complementary therapies, such as the ones in this book, if new drug therapies seem a distant possibility.

And then Alex leaves me with his most compelling takeaway. 'As I've gone to the field and become an expert in the space, my view of disease has fundamentally changed. I don't really think of it as disease any more. I really think of them as traits because we all live on this genetic spectrum. My genetic risk for bipolar disorder is not zero, even though

I've never been manic, so to say someone has the disease, versus doesn't, at the genetic level that doesn't quite add up. All the traits that we think about that are outside of disease are complex genetic traits,' he says, citing polygenic traits such as height and weight. 'Psychiatric conditions are not exceptional in that way. They're actually representative of most human traits,' he concludes. A reassuring way to reframe how we think of mental health.

● ● ●

Morning sunrays and leafy trees greet me as I virtually meet Dr Shebani Sethi Dalai at her home in Palo Alto, California. A psychiatrist, obesity doctor and professor, she is the founding director of the Metabolic Psychiatry Clinic at the Stanford University School of Medicine. Shebani talks to me about metabolic psychiatry, an emerging clinical discipline, and its impact on bipolar disorder, amongst other mental illnesses.

Weight gain is often an unfortunate, sometimes unavoidable, side effect of psychiatric medication, but Shebani questions what comes first. 'Are we developing psychiatric symptoms, such as depression, anxiety, psychosis, because there's essentially a metabolic dysfunction in the brain? Some research shows that there are deficits in energy metabolism in the brain. If we're thinking about metabolic reactions and processes, there is something that could be dysfunctional in the brain, which is then leading to the presentation of psychiatric symptoms. We don't have data necessarily that's showing causation. But we are seeing a lot of associations. Hypothetically, if there's a metabolic dysfunction, essentially causing the symptoms, then if we can reverse the dysfunction or bypass the dysfunction, then I would think that symptoms would improve. And so that's what I am studying and what my research is focused on. We just wrote a paper that details the different pathways and metabolic mechanisms as to why we think something abnormal is happening in energy metabolism for bipolar illness, and probably a lot of other mental illnesses as well,' she explains.

The exact science of metabolic psychiatry is a bit of a mouthful and well beyond the scope of this book, but it is best understood as an emerging discipline at the intersection of metabolism, metabolic dysfunction, nutrition and mental health. Not typical of standard psychiatric practice, Shebani says she merges her expertise in obesity medicine and psychiatry to take a full dietary history, does a physical exam, and looks at metabolic markers of her patients to treat the metabolic dysfunction as a way to improve mental health symptoms.

She advocates the ketogenic diet, where appropriate, to help treat metabolic dysfunction. 'This intervention can improve lipids, blood pressure, result in weight loss and is effective for obesity. It is a high-fat, moderate-protein, low-carbohydrate diet,' she says, adding that 'with mania, dopamine receptors can be really activated and excited. The ketogenic diet actually dampens down that response and can be helpful in these mood-states. If the ketogenic diet is actually helping with mood stabilization, making changes at the neurotransmitter level and energy production level, then you have a dietary intervention that's a tool like medication. What's fascinating is that the side effects are nothing in comparison to medication side effects and could even alleviate the medication side effects. However, more research needs to be done and I am not advocating for people to stop their medication. It saves lives, but we can begin to think about these additional tools for treatment intervention.'

She cites the example of one of her patients, who struggled with bipolar disorder and binge eating for most of her life, was on psychiatric medication, suffered from the disease of obesity and from severe chronic back pain. After being on a ketogenic diet over a period of two years, she lost weight, to the extent she was no longer categorized with obesity, was able to reduce some of her psychiatric medication, and felt notable improvements in her mood and quality of life. She stopped binge eating, the back pain vanished and she even felt her sexual libido awakening, resulting in more intimacy with her partner. A most promising way to reframe how we think about mental health.

● ● ●

Clinical psychologist and psychotherapist Narendra Kinger meets me in the conference room of the first Talk To Me centre, a 1000-square-foot walk-in clinic in an industrial estate in Mumbai's Mahim neighbourhood. The bright blue and white walls create an upbeat, yet professional ambience. Founded by Mr Kinger, Talk To Me strives to make mental health more accessible and inclusive, especially to the marginalized. We discuss the relationship between poverty and mental health and I leave promising to help him with expanding Talk To Me's donor base.

Talk To Me's outreach programmes include juveniles, children in vulnerable circumstances, women in shelter homes and trafficking survivors. Their interventions have enabled concerned authorities to take proactive corrective action by providing quantifiable evidence of mental health stressors amongst beneficiaries. Alcoholism, sexual trauma, a sense of hopelessness, livelihood concerns, unemployment and self-protection are some of the most common issues faced. The walk-in service at the Mahim centre also sees young adults and students who cannot otherwise afford therapy.

Professional therapy is out of reach for most Indians. 'Facilities are inadequate, infrastructure is inadequate, there are not enough professionals, people don't have money to pay for the service. It's a closed door. The poor don't have an option. That was the idea when we started Talk To Me. The key here is that poverty has a very important role to play in mental health. Poverty by itself is a contributory factor. I cannot take away poverty, I'm not a politician. But can I work on mental health? Yes, definitely,' he says.

'I think our job here is to give them a sense that somebody cares for you. Nobody has shown them that compassion. Talking to a concerned human being who's trying to help you, when you know that there's no ulterior motive, that itself is therapeutic,' he notices.

'Many of our physical health difficulties are related to psychological stress. Headaches, chest pain, breathing issues, acidity, muscular pain, lack of sleep, frequent vomiting, hair fall, deep pigmentation of the skin. If we can help calm you down, there are a lot of beneficial effects directly and indirectly to your overall physical health. So that's why therapy becomes important. I firmly believe that mental health is the next frontier of science for human beings to have a better life,' he professes.

Unaddressed mental health problems have a multiplier effect on society too, adversely impacting safety, employment, employability and the local economy. Therapy can address these, says Narendra.

'Safety is addressed by reduction in alienation, isolation, more understanding and teaching healthy coping mechanisms to individuals. Employment is impacted by increasing their connectedness to the world around them and improving learning skills, attention, motivation, goal-setting, etc. The local economy is boosted with reduction in crime, better family interactions, building of empathetic relationships, reduction of addictions, inclusivity as well as community support, fostering better ties amongst various sections of society. It is well known that poverty increases feelings of helplessness, meaninglessness and lack of control over one's life. Hence working on and addressing mental health issues at the bottom of the pyramid enhances the well-being of the community.'

The long-term vision is to establish Talk To Me centres across Mumbai, each accessible by public transport, making it easy for those at the bottom of the pyramid to access mental health services. A far-reaching approach to reframe how we think of mental health.

● ● ●

Dr Soumitra Pathare has a virtual background switched on when we connect over Zoom. He is working out of his study, he tells me. A psychiatrist and the director of the Pune-based Centre for Mental Health Law & Policy, Soumitra talks to me about Atmiyata, one of the Centre's most innovative, community-led mental healthcare projects.

Soumitra shares one of his favourite stories about Atmiyata's volunteer-led rural mental healthcare model. 'Our counselling sessions happen anywhere. One of our counsellors used to see a woman and they would do the counselling session whenever the woman went to the village well to draw water. They would meet and sit there for half an hour while she was drawing the water out, with the counsellor listening and talking to her. That's how it would take place.'

The anecdote illustrates Atmiyata's fundamental premise—that communities, especially tight-knit rural communities, are experts in their own contexts. Village volunteers are mentored and supervised by trained mental health facilitators to be counsellors. Called Atmiyata 'champions', they 'identify and provide primary support and counselling to persons with emotional stress and common mental health disorders and make referrals to the public health system in instances of severe mental illness, working through existing community groups to deliver these services,' describes a programme brochure. It goes on to say that the champions also facilitate access to social government benefits, make referrals for legal aid, shelter homes and employment generation, and build awareness, reduce stigma and enhance understanding of everyday social stressors. The programme is operational in over 500 villages in a rural district in the western Indian state of Gujarat and is expanding to other states within India.

The brochure and Soumitra emphasize that 'Atmiyata volunteers are informal caregivers and community members, not primary health workers, allowing for a high level of intervention by individuals who have a close connection with the social fabric of the place, share the living circumstances of persons needing care, and are able to communicate about mental health using context-specific and accessible language. Atmiyata's reliance on informal care by trained volunteers from the community lowers programme costs and helps in building trust.'

It is an organic, bottom-up process, run in close collaboration with the entire village. 'We go to the villages, we talk to the panchayats, we have a conversation with them. It's only if the sarpanch and the panchayat members agree that "yes, we want this programme here", then we will do it. Our champions have become locally quite well known. Gradually, everyone in the village knows that if you have any problem, you can go to the champion, they will help you out. We really wanted something that belonged to the community and started with the community. And so there was a sense of ownership to the whole process, which is what we've got now,' he says.

Scalability is built into the process through detailed manuals on training, mentoring and supervision. 'My colleagues hate it when I use the Subway or Pizza Hut analogy, but every single process has to be standardized and only then can you go down the social franchise route,' Soumitra laughs. The model can be replicated across the globe, he feels, especially in rural communities in low- and middle-income countries and, perhaps, in urban slums.

In fact, some community-led mental healthcare models originating in India are already making their way to the West. A model based on community healthcare workers, designed by the mental healthcare non-profit Sangath in Goa, is being adapted for rollout in Texas, in the United States, to make it contextually appropriate, says Dr Vikram Patel, the co-founder of Sangath.

The 'Pizza Hut' of community-led mental healthcare—an innovative way to reframe how we think of mental health.

● ● ●

Raj Mariwala is sitting in a high-backed, upholstered armchair when we meet virtually. A next-generation philanthropist and the director of the Mariwala Health Initiative, Raj supports and funds a range of mental health organizations, including researchers, activists, service providers, users and survivors, law and policy-makers and communities. We speak about a lot of issues!

Raj Mariwala counts the Queer Affirmative Counselling Practice as one of the most tangible achievements of the Mariwala Health Initiative. 'We run this programme personally. It is run by queer trans mental health professionals, to train psychologists, counsellors and psychiatrists on how to be queer-affirmative in their work, because there's no formal training given. The idea is to counter some of the more socially dominant narratives in mental health. About 250 mental health practitioners have been trained all over the country since 2019. We also have peer support practice work, where we hold a two-day workshop for people from within the community, to do peer practice, to have other people to talk to, to build support networks.'

The programme reflects two of Raj's core beliefs on mental health: highlighting intersectionality and focusing on the marginalized. 'I think what I am most proud of is probably having visibilized conversations around the intersectionality of mental health, as well as the linkages to people's contexts in terms of oppression. And this is discrimination on the basis of caste, class, gender, sexuality, ability. Having visibilized that from the vantage point, or from the point of power of a funder, is what is most important for us to have done. It's a continuous process,' she says.

For example, as a feminist, she questions the lack of linkage between the mental health movement and the women's movement. 'India has a very high number of housewives who die by suicide. Indian women die by suicide relatively far more than women do all over the world. So why aren't these linkages being made? Why hasn't the mental health activist movement allied with the women's movement? Why hasn't it allied with livelihood work? These are important questions to ask because they are directly related.'

Marginalization is also a very important consideration. 'When you build systems, if you build them for the centre and then try to reach the margins, you're going to take a very long time. If you build systems for the margins, reaching the centre is going to take much less time. And of course, looking at philanthropy as redistribution of wealth, these are the communities that we wanted to work with because they are the most in need. We do believe that philanthropy should be accountable to the larger populace and to the larger communities,' she summarizes.

The messages are unequivocal. Think of mental health as traits, not as disease. Make mental healthcare more accessible to the marginalized, whether through a clinic, outreach programmes, community volunteers or grant funding. And view mental healthcare through the lens of intersectionality.

In other words, mental health is about life—everyday life, for all of us. Mental health is about society—all aspects of it. We are all somewhere on the spectrum. Even though I began this book discussing statistics, of the percentage of a population officially diagnosed with a mental health condition, to think about mental health as divorced from our everyday realities—as individuals or as communities—is limited. It affects all of us, in profound and complex ways, at different times and stages of our lives. There is no progress without mental health and wellness.

And that should be the basis for future therapies.

Afterword
Letter from a Childhood Friend

Dear Aparna,

Thanks for sharing your manuscript with me. As one of your oldest schoolfriends, it's heartening for me to learn of your journey more closely. I would like to share my thoughts and responses to your book.

I walk away from this book with several takeaways. I believe this book can help anyone who's struggling, not just with bipolarity, mental health and chronic illness but also an existential crisis. It can help people navigate through life to become what they were meant to become through these different therapies or even 'life arenas', as I call them. I believe we were meant to live and express ourselves fully in all arenas of our life, not just in one or two.

You write a lot about purpose in this journey of self-realization. I think that purpose is perhaps that pattern, which is always uncovering itself. The question we can always keep asking ourselves is: 'What is the next stage of my unfolding?' It is ever dynamic and is evident mainly in hindsight. We may have a general sense, but we may not have this definitive thing, until we can actually look back and say, 'Ah, this was possibly the form the purpose was meant to take.'

I have also realized that when I consistently ask questions of myself it keeps me firmly grounded in my awareness and keeps me playfully present. When I ask myself questions it makes me aware of my innermost thoughts and feelings and the stories I live in. It helps me see that my experiences with the outside world echo my inner state. I am sometimes able to break away from personality traits and conditioning I don't like. And gradually this sort of thing has helped me to not take myself too seriously. I am amazed that your book too reflects this sort of curiosity and evolving consciousness. It's delightful to notice how two friends' journeys have paralleled in some ways—so unbeknownst to each other!

I enjoyed the gentleness with which you worked with yourself. At school you were confident, a go-getter, sometimes even aggressive to be honest. Then to read this book and see the intense self-work that you had to do, where you possibly lost such a sense of self-esteem and confidence! And how you gradually built yourself back—this discovery was surprising. I think the recognition that you needed to be gentle with yourself was probably one of the biggest enablers to your finding equilibrium.

Your journey resonated with me because I've been through many traumas myself recently and I realized that those traumas were actually about releasing layers of conditioning. In a simple line, your book is about how you release your conditioning and come to accept yourself. So, it was beautiful to read how you did it, because I was able to go back and view myself more kindly and not judge myself so much.

Another critical takeaway for me is that we heal through our inner work, but also very much in relationship with other people. They mirror us. We get to see different aspects of ourselves. And that enables healing. We get to see ourselves not in isolation, but in context. If we only take care of our physical body, our progress is lopsided. But these therapies you worked with are all interconnected. For example, something remarkable about your journey is that you've become a much more substantive giver. You opened yourself up to receive a lot and that positioned you so much more substantially to give. This is how life expresses itself, through these therapies, or 'life-arenas'.

I would like to leave you with two metaphors to represent bipolarity, or any mental health condition. Bipolarity is a constraint to which you needed to surrender. Surrender doesn't mean giving in, or acquiescing. It is almost the way you surrender to your guru: you allow the guru to lead you. You allowed bipolarity to teach you what it needed to teach you. The bipolarity became your guru, it gave you a roadmap for, in a sense, reaching for enlightenment. Something that you might think would take away your life, not allow you to survive, is the very thing that allowed you to reframe, turn around and gain life, helping you to explore your infinite potential as a human being.

Another metaphor is of dance. You have learnt to dance with your mental condition, with the help of your resources and therapists. To tango with your emotions, to go back and forth with small steps initially, until you feel resourced and are in rhythm, and can dance faster and faster without losing balance—that's something your journey reveals.

I loved the book, and I hope others will find it as helpful and moving as I did. All the best.

Much love,
Hetal Sheth

Closing Lines

To end, a few favourite lines that capture the essence of my attitude to life when I'm feeling positive, and especially as a reminder when I'm feeling low of how we can be happy for no reason.

'The 59th Street Bridge Song (Feelin' Groovy)'
Slow down, you move too fast
You got to make the morning last
Just kicking down the cobblestones
Looking for fun and feeling groovy'
—Paul Simon and Art Garfunkel

'You can't wait until life isn't hard anymore before you decide to be happy.'
—Nightbirde

'Love You Zindagi'
'Main thodi si moody hoon
Tu thodi si tedi hai
Kya khoob ye jodi hai
Teri meri'
—Kausar Munir

Mental Health Resources

If you or your loved ones are looking for access to free therapy/counselling sessions with trained mental health professionals, you can reach out to the helplines mentioned below.

- **iCALL**
  Helpline: 9152987821
  Time: 10 a.m. to 8 p.m. | Monday to Saturday
  Languages: English, Hindi, Marathi, Bengali, Gujarati and Tamil.

iCALL is a psychosocial helpline for individuals in emotional and psychological distress. They provide professional and free counselling through technology-assisted mediums such as telephone, email and chat to anyone in need of emotional support, irrespective of age, gender, sexual orientation or race, and transcending geographical distances while ensuring confidentiality.

- **Mann Talks**
  Helpline: 8686139139
  Time: 9 a.m. to 8 p.m. | Monday to Sunday
  Languages: English, Hindi and Marathi

A Shantilal Shanghvi Foundation initiative, Mann Talks focuses on empowering individuals to take charge of their mental health. A team of trained mental health professionals offers an empathetic and non-judgemental environment where one can share their thoughts, emotions and experiences freely. They guide individuals in making informed decisions about their mental health.

- **BMC–Mpower 1 on 1**
  Helpline: 1800-120-820050
  Time: 24/7
  Languages: English, Hindi and Marathi

In order to deal with the mental health concerns arising out of the pandemic and subsequent lockdowns, the BMC and Mpower 1 on 1, along with the Government of Maharashtra, have started a toll-free, 24/7 helpline that helps individuals sail through the lockdowns by addressing their concerns.

- **Talk To Me**
  Helpline: 8484929124, 8591238886, 8591231945, 9321811294, 8591250096
  Time: 9.30 a.m. to 6.30 p.m. | Monday to Saturday
  Languages: English, Hindi, Marathi, Gujarati, Sindhi and Urdu

Founded by clinical psychologist and psychotherapist Narendra Kinger, Mumbai-based Talk To Me provides counselling services free of cost to those who cannot pay for therapy, and pay-as-you-can counselling services at affordable charges, at its walk-in centre in Mahim as well as virtually. Its goal is to make mental health services accessible and inclusive.

If you or one of your loved ones are experiencing a mental health crisis and need of immediate psychosocial support, please reach out to the helplines mentioned below.

- **Vandrevala Foundation**
  Helpline: 9999666555 | WhatsApp: 0256-6662142
  Time: 24/7
  Languages: English, Hindi, Gujarati, Marathi, Tulu, Tamil, Telugu, Malayalam, Kannada, Odia and Bengali

The Cyrus and Priya Vandrevala Foundation is a non-profit organization that aims to provide significant funding and aid contributions for those suffering from mental health problems and illnesses in India. The 24/7 mental health helpline aims to aid patients, their relatives and others struggling with mental health problems. The helpline currently operates pan India. Counselling is also available through chat, email and WhatsApp directly from the website.

- **Kiran Mental Health Helpline**
  Helpline: 1800-599-0019
  Time: 24/7
  Languages: Hindi, Assamese, Tamil, Marathi, Odia, Telugu, Malayalam, Gujarati, Punjabi, Kannada, Bengali, Urdu and English

Launched by the Ministry of Social Justice and Empowerment, Kiran is a 24/7 toll-free helpline set up to provide support to

people facing anxiety, stress, depression, suicidal thoughts
and other mental health concerns.

- **Roshni Trust**
  Helpline: 040-66202000, 040-66202001
  Time: 11 a.m. to 9 p.m. | All days of the week
  Languages: English, Hindi, Telugu and Urdu

Roshni trust is a voluntary organization that values human
life. Roshni helpline comes under its umbrella. Roshni
helpline provides free and confidential service by providing
emotional support to the depressed and the suicidal.

- **Connecting Trust**
  Helpline: 9922001122, 9922004305
  Time: 12 p.m. to 8 p.m. | All days of the week
  Languages: English, Hindi and Marathi

Connecting Trust is a non-judgemental, non-advisory,
confidential and anonymous space for those feeling low,
distressed and/or suicidal.

- **Parivarthan**
  Helpline: 7676602602
  Time: 1 p.m. to 10 p.m. | Monday to Friday
  Languages: English, Hindi, Punjabi, Marathi, Haryanvi,
  Kannada, Tamil and Bengali

Parivarthan Counselling, Training and Research Centre is
a registered, non-profit society that provides multimodal
services in the field of mental health (www.parivarthan.org).
The helpline is serviced by trained, professional counsellors
who are committed to a rigorously ethical practice and who
respect the confidentiality of the callers.

- **Mitram Foundation**
  Helpline: 080-25722573
  Time: 10 a.m. to 4 p.m. | All days of the week
  Languages: English and Hindi

Mitram Foundation is a suicide prevention helpline that aims to offer emotional support to those going through a crisis in their lives, especially the distressed, depressed and suicidal.

If you can afford therapy and are looking to find a therapist, you can log on to any of the following websites that are aggregating and/or vetting mental health professionals.

- Therapize India (https://www.therapizeindia.com/)
- Live Love Laugh Foundation (https://www. thelivelovelaughfoundation.org/)
- Mind Clan (https://themindclan.com/)
- iCALL's crowdsourced list of mental health professionals (https://www.facebook.com/435423836519798/ posts/1663493417046161/)

If you are struggling with your own mental health or are a caregiver looking for support groups, group therapy or sharing spaces that cater to various communities and mental health needs across India, you can explore the options listed in the websites below.

- Mind Clan provides an aggregated list (https:// themindclan.com/)
- Therapize India (https://www.therapizeindia.com/)
- BecauseYOU (https://www.becauseyou.in/)
- Caregiver Saathi (https://caregiversaathi.co.in/)
- Institute of Psychological Health, Pune (https:// iphpune.org/)

- Schizophrenia Awareness Association, Pune (https://schizophrenia.org.in /)
- Manav Foundation, Mumbai (https://www.manavfoundation.org.in/)
- Bipolar India (https://bipolarindia.com/)
- The White Elephant Women's Support Group (https://www.hemangivyawahare.com)
- The Alt Story (http://alternativestory.in/announcing-support-groups/)

If you are looking for website or application-based resources for more information on mental health or mindfulness, you can explore the options listed below.

Websites
- Beyond Blue (https://www.beyondblue.org.au/)
- White Swan Foundation (https://www.whiteswanfoundation.org/)
- Mann Talks (www.manntalks.org)
- Inner Space (https://innerspacetherapy.in/mindfulness-programs/)

Apps
- Ten Percent Happier
- Calm
- 7 Cups
- InnerHour
- Headspace
- Wysa

Acknowledgements

A ny memoirist, and particularly one living with a mental health condition like me, has at least two major constituencies to thank—the individuals who help us live our lives, and the ones who help us find our voice, and turn it into a book. (Many of these gems overlap, of course).

I began making a list of the those who help me live my life before I wrote a single word of this manuscript. It was long. So I would like to simply thank my precious 'tribe of therapists'; all those mentioned in this book and those who wish to remain invisible. I hope you know that you are the reason I say that mental health is a team sport.

The list of those who helped me turn my ideas into a book is just as treasured.

Anand Mahindra, thank you for the foreword (again!).

Thank you to those who read my early drafts—Seema Bhangar, Jim Downing, Hetal Sheth, Ankita Patel, Gayatri Kotikalapudi, Upasana Makati, Ami Goda, Abhijit Avasthi, Moomal Mehta, Saumya Roy, Sonya Dutta Choudhary and my writers' club for your invaluable suggestions, notes and conversations.

A huge thank you to Mary Abdo and the Bombay Feminist Book Club, where the book was conceived.

I could not have asked for a more thorough, diligent and committed research associate than Kriti Krishnan, a partner in all mental health explorations.

Or a better sponsor and friend than Eric Nestler at Mount Sinai, thank you for your generosity and wisdom.

Mithun Thanks and Sangeetha Ganesh, thank you for your assistance on legal issues.

Thank you Urmila Ramakrishna, Elizabeth Virkar, Ms Braganza, Tuli Patel, Lily Maneckji, Helen Mathur and Patricia Powell, just some of my many English teachers for helping a wordsmith discover her trade.

Seema Chowdhry, my decade-long editor at the *Mint*, and Khozem Merchant, my writing mentor, you honed my craft with patience, encouragement and lots of green tea.

Namita Gokhale and Chiki Sarkar, thank you for believing that I had it in me to step back and tell my story.

Muskan Bubna and Darsh Bhatela, you breathe life into my words with your visual artistry.

Ruchita and Surabhi Sharma, thank you for being my allies on this journey of spreading the mental health gospel. Here's to the sisterhood!

I am incredibly grateful to Rukmini Chawla Kumar, my wonderful agent, and the entire team at Penguin Random House India, including Akangksha Sarmah, the book's talented cover designer; Roshini Dadlani, my first commissioning editor; Gurveen Chadha, my fabulous executive editor; Radhika Agarwal, my meticulous copy editor; Prateek Agarwal, my dynamic lead publicist; Aishvarya Misra, my responsive digital publicist, Vijesh Kumar, the most committed sales head, Natasha Kapur, the most motivated marketing head, and Milee Ashwarya, my trusted friend and publisher; for this opportunity.

Most of all, I would like to thank those who help me make sense of my chemical khichdi every day—my immediate and extended family, the Piramals, Rajes and Kejriwals. And my daily download friends—Pooja Samtani, Seema Bhangar, Upasana Makati, Ankita Patel and Saumya Lashkari. Thank you for being there for me, every single day. I hope I reciprocate your love and affection.

This book was written during the pandemic, and I would like to say a special thanks to everyone, from care workers to delivery boys, who keep us safe.

And finally, I would like to close with a prayer to a higher power, and express my deep gratitude for a multitude of blessings.

Notes

Foreword

1. World Health Organization. Mental Health Burden. https://www.who.int/health-topics/mental-health#tab=tab_2
2. Hannah. 2018. 'Global Mental Health: Five Key Insights which Emerge from the Data'. Our World in Data. 16 May 2018. https://ourworldindata.org/global-mental-health#licence
3. Douglas. 2020. '5 Things to Know About Mental Health Across the World'. World Economic Forum. 9 October 2020. https://www.weforum.org/agenda/2020/10/mental-health-day-covid19-coronavirus-global/

Introduction

1. 'COVID-19 Blues: Suicidal Thoughts on the Rise in Youth, Say Therapists'. The CSR Journal. 15 September 2020. https://thecsrjournal.in/covid-19-blues-survey-mental-health-india/
2. Ibid.
3. Joel P. Joseph, 'COVID-19 and Mental Health: Suicidal Tendencies and Self-Harm on the Rise'. The Wire. 24 July 2020, https://thewire.in/health/covid-19-mental-health-suicidal-tendencies-self-harm-rise

Part I: The Condition

Chapter 1. Un-Diagnosis (2000–2012)

1. Durrell, Gerald. 1956. *My Family & Other Animals*. Penguin Group: Puffin books.
2. Jamison, Kay R. 1995. *An Unquiet Mind: A Memoir of Moods and Madness*. Pan Macmillan: Picador.
3. American Psychiatric Association. Bipolar Disorders. https://www.psychiatry.org/patients-families/bipolar-disorders/what-are-bipolar-disorders
4. Ibid.
5. Ibid.
6. Ibid.
7. Ibid.
8. Lancet Psychiatry. 2020. 'The Burden of Mental Disorders Across the States of India: The Global Burden of Disease Study 1990-2017'. The Lancet Psychiatry Journal Vol. 7. February 2020 (14861) https://www.thelancet.com/journals/lanpsy/article/PIIS2215-0366(19)30475-4/fulltext
9. Ibid.
10. JCO Global Oncology. 2020. 'Cancer Statistics, 2020: Report From National Cancer Registry Programme, India'. July 6:1063-1075. doi: 10.1200/GO.20.00122 or: https://ascopubs.org/doi/pdf/10.1200/GO.20.00122.
11. Gururaj G., Varghese M., Benegal V., Rao G.N., Pathak K., Singh L.K., Mehta R.Y., Ram D., Shibukumar T.M., Kokane A., Lenin Singh R.K., Chavan B.S., Sharma P., Ramasubramanian C., Dalal P.K., Saha P.K., Deuri S.P., Giri A.K., Kavishvar A.B., Sinha V.K., Thavody J., Chatterji R., Akoijam B.S., Das S., Kashyap A., Ragavan V.S., Singh S.K., Misra R. and NMHS collaborators group. 'National Mental Health Survey of India, 2015-16: Prevalence, Patterns and Outcomes'. Bengaluru, National Institute of Mental Health and Neuro Sciences, NIMHANS Publication No. 129, 2016. https://nimhans.ac.in/national-mental-health-survey/

12. World Health Organization. Mental Health Burden. https://www.who.int/health-topics/mental-health#tab=tab_2

13. Douglas. 2020. '5 Things to Know About Mental Health Across the World'. World Economic Forum. 9 October 2020. https://www.weforum.org/agenda/2020/10/mental-health-day-covid19-coronavirus-global/

14. Cerullo, Michael A., and Stephen M. Strakowski. 'The Prevalence and Significance of Substance Use Disorders in Bipolar Type I and II Disorder'. Substance Abuse Treatment, Prevention, and Policy Vol. 2 29. 1 October 2007. doi:10.1186/1747-597X-2-2 OR https://www.ncbi.nlm.nih.gov/pmc/articles/PMC2094705/

15. Nevatia, Shreevatsa. 2017. *How To Travel Light: My Memories of Madness and Melancholia.* Penguin Books.

16. Greenberg, Michael. 2009. *Hurry Down Sunshine: A Father's Memoir of Love and Madness.* Bloomsbury.

Chapter 2. Me vs Me (2013–2018)

1. American Psychiatric Association. 2015. *Understanding Mental Disorders: Your Guide to DSM-5.* American Psychiatric Publishing.

2. Ibid.

3. Gururaj G., Varghese M., Benegal V., Rao G.N., Pathak K., Singh L.K., Mehta R.Y., Ram D., Shibukumar T.M., Kokane A., Lenin Singh R.K., Chavan B.S., Sharma P., Ramasubramanian C., Dalal P.K., Saha P.K., Deuri S.P., Giri A.K., Kavishvar A.B., Sinha V.K., Thavody J., Chatterji R., Akoijam B.S., Das S., Kashyap A., Ragavan V.S., Singh S.K., Misra R. and NMHS collaborators group. 'National Mental Health Survey of India, 2015-16: Prevalence, Patterns and Outcomes'. Bengaluru, National Institute of Mental Health and Neuro Sciences, NIMHANS Publication No. 129, 2016. https://nimhans.ac.in/national-mental-health-survey/

4. Ibid.

5. Ibid.

6. Sarah Owen and Amanda Saunders. 2008. *Bipolar Disorder -The Ultimate Guide*. Oneworld Publications.
7. Aparna Piramal Raje, 'Year-End Special: In Search of My Old Self', *Mint*, 29 December 2017, https://www.livemint.com/Leisure/vS8DqgPJbtVF5GHKvrLlLO/In-search-of-my-old-self.html
8. Schweig, Graham M. 2007. *Bhagavad Gita: The Beloved Lord's Secret Love Song*. HarperCollins Publishers: HarperOne
9. Ibid.

Chapter 3. Equilibrium . . . and Covid-19 (2018–present)

1. Leader, Darian. 2013. *Strictly Bipolar*. Penguin Books.
2. Ibid.
3. Ibid.
4. Ibid.

Part II: The Seven Therapies
Chapter 4. Medical Therapies: Accepting the Difference between Personality and Illness

1. Wang, Philip S. et al. 'Delays in Initial Treatment Contact After First Onset of a Mental Disorder'. Health Services Research Vol. 39,2 (2004): 393-415. doi:10.1111/j.1475-6773.2004.00234.x
2. Gururaj G., Varghese M., Benegal V., Rao G.N., Pathak K., Singh L.K., Mehta R.Y., Ram D., Shibukumar T.M., Kokane A., Lenin Singh R.K., Chavan B.S., Sharma P., Ramasubramanian C., Dalal P.K., Saha P.K., Deuri S.P., Giri A.K., Kavishvar A.B., Sinha V.K., Thavody J., Chatterji R., Akoijam B.S., Das S., Kashyap A., Ragavan V.S., Singh S.K., Misra R. and NMHS collaborators group. 'National Mental Health Survey of India, 2015-16: Prevalence, Patterns and Outcomes'. Bengaluru, National Institute of Mental Health and Neuro Sciences, NIMHANS Publication No. 129, 2016. https://nimhans.ac.in/national-mental-health-survey/

3.   Ibid.
4.   Patel J., Marwaha R. 2021. *Akathisia*. StatPearls Publishing. https://www.ncbi.nlm.nih.gov/books/NBK519543/
5.   Parial, S. 'Bipolar Disorder in Women'. Indian Journal of Psychiatry 2015;57, Suppl S2:252-63. https://www.indianjpsychiatry.org/text.asp?2015/57/6/252/161488
6.   Kalpana Sharma, 'We Need More Mental Health Care Professionals in India'. *The Times of India*. 10 October 2018, https://timesofindia.indiatimes.com/life-style/health-fitness/health-news/we-need-more-mental-health-care-professionals-in-india/articleshow/66146320.cms

Chapter 5. Love Therapy: Mental Health Is a Team Sport

1.   Chadda, Rakesh K. 'Caring for the Family Caregivers of Persons with Mental Illness'. Indian Journal of Psychiatry Vol. 56,3 (2014): 221-7. doi:10.4103/0019-5545.140616
2.   Chadda, Rakesh K. 'Caring for the Family Caregivers of Persons with Mental Illness'. Indian Journal of Psychiatry Vol. 56,3 (2014): 221-7. doi:10.4103/0019-5545.140616 citing Magliano L., Fiorillo A., De Rosa C., Malangone C., Maj M. National Mental Health Project Working Group. 'Family Burden in Long-term Diseases: A Comparative Study in Schizophrenia vs. Physical Disorders'. Soc Sci Med. 2005;61:313–22.
3.   Varalakshmi Vemuru and Samhita Kumar, 'The Unheard Voices of Women Caregivers for People with Mental Illness', World Bank Blogs, May 16, 2017, https://blogs.worldbank.org/endpovertyinsouthasia/unheard-voices-women-caregivers-people-mental-illness

Chapter 6. Allies and the Therapy of Empathy

1.   Van Der Kolk, Bessel. 2015. *The Body Keeps the Score: Brain, Mind, and Body in the Healing of Trauma*. Penguin Books.

2.   Putnam, Robert D. 'Bowling Alone: America's Declining
      Social Capital.' Journal of Democracy 6, no. 1 (1995): 65-78.
      doi:10.1353/jod.1995.0002.
3.   Waldinger, Robert. 2015. 'What Makes a Good Life? Lessons
      from the Longest Study on Happiness'. Uploaded on 25
      January 2016. TedxBeaconStreet. https://www.ted.com/
      talks/robert_waldinger_what_makes_a_good_life_lessons_
      from_the_longest_study_on_happiness?language=en
4.   Ibid.
5.   Ibid.
6.   Ibid.
7.   Ibid.
8.   Ibid.

Chapter 7. Work Therapy and Playing Opposite-Handed

1.   Gururaj G., Varghese M., Benegal V., Rao G.N., Pathak K.,
      Singh L.K., Mehta R.Y., Ram D., Shibukumar T.M., Kokane A.,
      Lenin Singh R.K., Chavan B.S., Sharma P., Ramasubramanian
      C., Dalal P.K., Saha P.K., Deuri S.P., Giri A.K., Kavishvar
      A.B., Sinha V.K., Thavody J., Chatterji R., Akoijam B.S., Das
      S., Kashyap A., Ragavan V.S., Singh S.K., Misra R. and NMHS
      collaborators group. 'National Mental Health Survey of India,
      2015-16: Prevalence, Patterns and Outcomes'. Bengaluru,
      National Institute of Mental Health and Neuro Sciences,
      NIMHANS Publication No. 129, 2016. https://nimhans.
      ac.in/national-mental-health-survey/
2.   World Health Organization 2005. Mental Health Policy
      and Service Guidance Package. 'Mental Health Policies and
      Programmes in the Workplace'. https://www.who.int/
      mental_health/policy/workplace_policy_programmes.pdf
3.   'All in the Mind: The State of Mental Health in Corporate
      India'. 2020. https://in.gigroup.com/all-in-the-mind-the-
      state-of-mental-health-in-corporate-india/

4. Bloom, D.E., Cafiero-Fonseca E.T., Candeias V., Adashi E.,Bloom L., Gurfein L., Jané-Llopis E., Lubet A., Mitgang E., Carroll O'Brien J., Saxena A. 2014. 'Economics of Non-Communicable Diseases in India: The Costs and Returns on Investment of Interventions to Promote Healthy Living and Prevent, Treat, and Manage NCDs'. World Economic Forum, Harvard School of Public Health. http://www3.weforum.org/docs/WEF_EconomicNonCommunicableDiseasesIndia_Report_2014.pdf

Chapter 8. Self-Therapy: Conversations on Identity, Purpose and Dharma

1. Schweig, Graham M. 2007. *Bhagavad Gita: The Beloved Lord's Secret Love Song*. HarperCollins Publishers: HarperOne.
2. Solomon, Andrew. 2015. *The Noonday Demon: An Atlas of Depression*. Simon & Schuster: Scribner.

Chapter 9. The Life-Changing Tributaries of Spiritual Therapy

1. Schweig, Graham M. 2007. *Bhagavad Gita: The Beloved Lord's Secret Love Song*. HarperCollins Publishers: HarperOne.
2. Russell Rodgers, 'The Four Dharmas of Gampopa'. Shambhala Times. 15 September 2016, https://shambhalatimes.org/2016/09/15/the-four-dharmas-of-gampopa/
3. The Altruist. 2007. http://thealtruist.org/dava-dua-program/
4. Ibid.
5. Varalakshmi, 'Dawa-Dua: How Medical Treatment Complements Prayer for People with Mental Illness in India'. World Bank Blogs. 3 November 2016, https://blogs.worldbank.org/endpovertyinsouthasia/dawa-dua-how-medical-treatment-complements-prayer-people-mental-illness-india

Chapter 10. Lifestyle Therapy: Attending to the Garden of Mental Wellness

1. Jones, Steven, Peter Hayward and Dominic Lam. 2009. *Coping with Bipolar Disorder: A CBT-Informed Guide to Living with Manic Depression.* Oneworld Books.

2. Jamison, Kay R. 1995. *An Unquiet Mind: A Memoir of Moods and Madness.* Pan Macmillan: Picador.

3. Walker, Matthew. 2017. *Why We Sleep: The New Science of Sleep and Dreams.* Penguin Books.

4. Ibid.

5. Mayer, Emeran. *The Mind-Gut Connection: How the Hidden Conversation Within Our Bodies Impacts Our Mood, Our Choices, and Our Overall Health.* 2016. HarperCollins Publishers: Harper Wave.

6. Brown, Stuart with Christopher Vaughan. 2009. *Play: How It Shapes the Brain, Opens the Imagination, and Invigorates the Soul.* Penguin Group: Avery.

7. Ibid.

Part III: Conclusion
Chapter 11. Reflections on Mental Health

1. The Financial Review. 2020. 'Warren Buffett: "Volatility Does Not Measure Risk"' Uploaded on 9 January 2020. YouTube video. https://www.youtube.com/watch?v=KmQk4zkrdzU